Pre-School Play

PRE-SCHOOL PLAY

Kenneth Jameson
and Pat Kidd

VNR VAN NOSTRAND REINHOLD COMPANY New York

Acknowledgements

Some of the ideas in the section on sound and music are gratefully acknowledged to David Evans, Primary Schools Music Adviser to the Inner London Education Authority.

The authors' thanks are also due to Community Playthings, Robertsbridge, Sussex for permission to reproduce figure 44, and to James Galt & Co. Ltd, Cheadle, Cheshire, for permission to reproduce figure 37.

Van Nostrand Reinhold Regional Offices:
New York   Cincinnati   Chicago   Millbrae   Dallas

Van Nostrand Reinhold International Offices:
London   Toronto   Melbourne

Copyright © 1974 by Kenneth Jameson and Pat Kidd

Library of Congress Cataloging in Publication Data

Jameson, Kenneth.
 Pre-school play.

 Bibliography: p. 108
 1. Education, Preschool – Handbooks, manuals, etc.
 2. Play – Handbooks, manuals, etc.   I. Kidd, Patricia, joint author.   II. Title.
 LB1140.2.J35   372.21   73-19562
 ISBN 0-442-24430-2

All rights reserved. No part of this work covered by the copyright hereon may be reproduced or used in any form or by any means – graphic, electronic, or mechanical, including photocopying, recording, taping, or information storage and retrieval systems – without written permission of the publisher.

Printed in Great Britain

Published by Van Nostrand Reinhold Company
A Division of Litton Educational Publishing, Inc.
450 West 33rd Street, New York N.Y. 10001

Contents

Foreword   6
Playgroups   7
Play   8
Fantasy   11
Basic activities   12
Painting and drawing   13
Clay, play-dough, and plasticine   30
Woodwork   36
Printing table   37
Experimenting with junk   39
Collage and sticky table   41
Cooking   45
Magic   47
Building   55
Sound and music   60
Literary activities   66
Games of fantasy   72
Jig-saw puzzles   78
Interest tables   81
Nature   88
Fiddle-board   91
Outings   93
Physical activities   95
Language   98
Practicalities   101
Present and future   106
Books, films and addresses   108
Index   112

Foreword

Patricia Kidd and Kenneth Jameson are no strangers to children or playgroups, and they have a warm sympathy for parents. We bring our children into the world with pride, joy, wonder and love, and then our confidence is apt to falter as we realize that we don't know too much about children. We think back to our own childhood, at home and at school, and we try to reproduce what we enjoyed and avoid what we disliked.

In *Pre-School Play* the authors help us to offer children experiences that may not be found in many people's memories, and the explanations of how and why to set about this are so convincing that we feel impelled to try them out, and then to 'stand back and observe'. Even if our own childhood experiences fell far short of those being advocated for today's children, the illustrations and children's quotations ring true and suggest that there is more to play than meets the eye: we are prepared to agree that 'magic for most of us is in short supply. Let us not deny it to the children.' This book arouses a confident desire to try to offer the magic of real play to children, and in doing so we shall become aware of the magic of childhood, which is a state in its own right needing to be lived and enjoyed to the full.

Brenda Crowe
National Adviser to the
Pre-School Playgroups Association

Playgroups

The National Pre-School Playgroups Association was formed in 1961 after Belle Tutaev (mother of a three-year-old) wrote a letter to a national newspaper. Through the letter she asked if mothers who shared her concern over the lack of nursery school provision would join her in a petition to the Ministry of Education. She also suggested that while waiting for government action, mothers should make their own provision. She received over 3,500 enthusiastic replies and soon after this PPA was formed.

Other organizations, in particular Save the Children Fund, are concerned with playgroups, and the word is used to describe many and varied forms of provision for under-fives. In this book the word refers to groups which are of ten to twenty children and meet together three to five times a week under the supervision of two or three adults. At least one of the adults will usually have attended a playgroup workers' course. They meet sometimes in a private house but more usually in the local church hall or community hall. Some branches of PPA now receive grants from their Local Education Authority to employ playgroup advisers and some groups receive grants towards equipment and running expenses from their Department of Social Services. However, in many cases, the parents are totally responsible for the finances of the playgroup. This usually means they have to raise funds to cover rent, wages and provision of play equipment plus materials.

Playgroups are designed to provide play activities which not only amuse children, but provide a means for them to develop a familiarity with the world around them. These activities include sand, water, paint, clay, jig-saws, construction toys, books, home-corner, dressing-up clothes and climbing apparatus. The children are also offered experience in music and storytelling.

Although this book deals mainly with providing play for children in a group, parents who read it will find it perfectly possible to provide many of the activities at home.

Play

Play, according to the *Oxford Dictionary*, is 'to move about in lively or capricious manner, frisk, flit, flutter, pass gently around, alternate rapidly...'

That definition will touch a chord in all who have to deal with very young children, whether at home or in the playgroup. It does not, however, say very much about the nature of play. 'To play with the child' often implies 'to amuse the child'. 'The child is playing' is taken to mean he is entertaining himself. There is much more to it than that. Play is a significant activity.

The play of the very young child has much in common with the play of young animals. The lion cub's playful tussles with his fellow cub are a preparation for the more serious defensive battles to come. Their hide-and-seek game will change, before long, into the vital hunt for food to enable them to survive. The child in the high chair, illustrated in fig. 1, is not merely amusing herself. She too is preparing herself for later life. But how, and what, exactly, is she doing?

We will leave aside, for the moment, how the blackcurrant juice found its way on to her chair tray. The liquid is bright crimson. It makes a noticeable contrast with the white tray. The child's eye is attracted to it. She sees it. Having looked at it for a moment, with her arms half-raised, she slowly lowers her fingers and touches it. It is cold and wet. Study her expression. She likes the feel of it. She moves her fingers about and in so doing she changes the shape of the blob of colour.

To manipulate a blob of colour on a white ground, whether it is blackcurrant on a white tray or paint on a white canvas, is to paint.

The adult reaction to the above childish activity may well be 'Oh! *What* a mess,' or 'Don't play with your food'; but the child is not just playing with her food, making a mess. She is beginning to explore her environment, through a play situation. She begins by responding to a visual experience, of the colour of the blackcurrant juice. She continues by exploring what she sees through the sense of touch, with her fingers. Her fingers move. The shape of colour changes. She observes the changing shapes. She finds the process pleasant and her facial expression reveals her pleasure. Even at this age the child will explore any and every situation in which he, or she, finds himself.

As he grows older his visual reactions, his instinct to explore, his inborn curiosity, his instinct to experiment with everything in every conceivable way, will increase steadily. As a result he develops his awareness, his faculties, his responses; and he becomes familiar with his environment.

It is necessary now to say how the blackcurrant juice got on to the child's tray. It was deliberately put there by an adult who knew in advance, before he did it, what the child's reactions would be. He poured it on knowing what would happen, and he did it in order to get the photograph which is shown in the illustration. The situation was set up for the child by an adult who knew what the likely result would be. It contains the germ of all that is to happen in the playgroup. The playgroup should be planned as a place where children can meet together, where they can find situations, set up by experienced adults, in which childish curiosity can be satisfied, childish imagination can be exercised, childish ingenuity can be encouraged, muscles can be stretched and strengthened, sensitivities can be developed, where in a word the child's natural instincts can be given free rein in appropriate situations, with known and predictable beneficial results.

Provide a tricycle and the child will ride it. Put climbing apparatus and he will climb. Put paint and he will explore it, find out what it will do and will use it. Children are naturally, instinctively and irresistibly drawn into activity by curiosity, fascination, fantasy. They do not need to be shown or taught.

Fig. 1

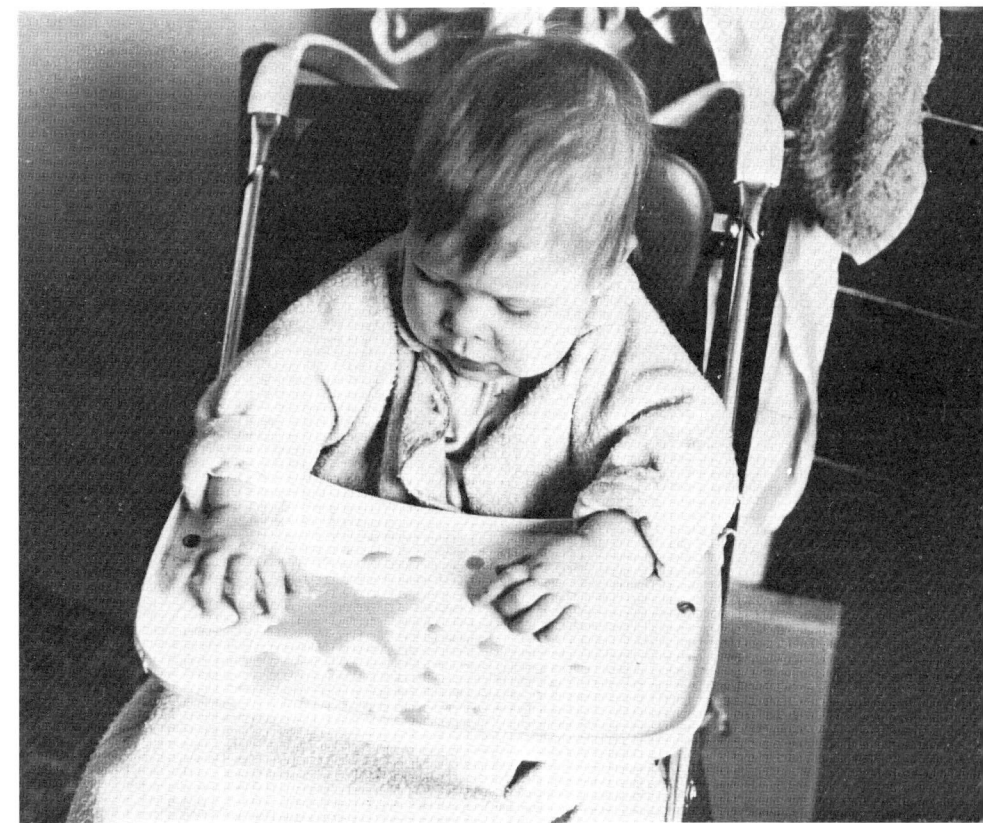

The adult's role is to provide suitable situations and then stand back, not to interfere, or teach, or over-persuade, but to be on hand, to show interest and provide encouragement when appropriate.

This book deals with the range of play situations possible and desirable in the playgroup, and some of the practical problems and human considerations involved in providing these. It also describes some of the experiences which may arise out of the children's involvement, visual experiences, tactile experiences, development of powers of imagination and, most important, the opportunity to indulge in fantasy.

The young child lives his life in a context of play. So, when does play cease to be play and become work? Should this happen? Is it the teacher and the parent who create the distinction? Camilla came home from infant reception class (nursery school), on the first day, and announced, 'We work in the morning and play in the afternoon.'

Fantasy

We all have a bit of the Walter Mitty in our make-up. Some of us have a lot more than others. A holiday advertisement may spark off a day dream of a stroll along the edge of the iridescent foam on a golden beach hand in hand with a glamorous partner. This dream state, this imagining, is fantasy, and it plays a more significant part in our lives than many people realize. The normal adult is usually aware of his fantasies. He differentiates clearly between fantasy and reality. The child, and especially the very young child, on the other hand, is aware of no such distinction. He continually alternates between real life and fantasy. For a period he is in the fantasy world and then he goes back to the real world. In the real world he is totally awake and aware, talking to the adult, taking action. In his fantasy life he may be totally unaware of his mother and father and his surroundings. He may not hear, or take notice, if he is spoken to. This is not because he is deliberately ignoring his surroundings and the people around him. It is because, for the time being, he is unaware of them. The fantasy has taken over and that which he is imagining in his mind has become more real to him than the real world surrounding him. Every adult whether parent, teacher, nurse, social worker, or playgroup worker, should know about the child's dual existence, in the two worlds of fantasy and reality. Most difficulties in dealing with very young children arise from a lack of such knowledge.

Next time you are in the company of a three- or four-year-old, watch him. Suppose he is holding a small cardboard box in his hand. At one moment he will be talking to you. The next moment he will be pushing the box along the edge of the table: 'It's a truck, the man is going to get the sand for the buildings.' He pushes the box round a plate, 'It's going round the island'; 'There's a steep hill. The brakes have broken; it's going to crash; *Crash!! Bang!!*' The game will totally absorb him while it lasts. He will be oblivious of you. From being physically present in the physical world the child has crossed over into being magically present in the world of his own imagination, and on each occasion when this happens, at each new imagining, his powers of make-believe will grow and develop. Imagination is a storehouse of ideas. It inspires speech, enlarges vocabulary, facilitates communication, develops the artistic sense, makes personal relations easier and supports creative thinking.

We do well if we can develop the child's powers of imagination.

The contents of this book, under the various headings, give details of play situations appropriate at home and in the playgroup. They all take account of the child's natural interests and characteristics. In all of them the possibilities for developing powers of imagination, in terms of fantasy, are discussed. The games of fantasy in which the child engages are a major factor in helping the adult to understand the child.

Basic activities

For the 0 to 5 year old with whom we are dealing, there are certain basic activities which are equally suitable for both home and playgroup. In both, when setting up the play situation, it is wise to concentrate, at first, upon these basic activities. They are: painting, drawing, sand, water, clay, dough, home-corner, climbing, building blocks, books.

Painting and drawing

Scribbling and dabbling with colour are two of the earliest manifestations of play activities. Scribble play leads first to making lines and then to primitive drawing. Dabbling with paint leads to blob-making and arranging, and then to patches and finally to painted patterns in colour. The drawing and the painting proceed in orderly sequence. We will look at both these sequences taking scribble-play first and dabbling second.

The scribble–line–drawing sequence

In order to form a better understanding of play situations at home and in the playgroup we must know how the young child discovers and develops play techniques in the years before he enters the playgroup, in other words up to the age of three. He begins very early, as we have seen with the example of the blackcurrant purée, and it is a continuing process. Play with drawing and painting is particularly important because it leaves behind visible, assessable, evidence on easel, or paper, or wall! By means of such evidence we can observe aspects of the child's stages of development.

The high-chair situation described earlier is a clear example of the child's developing a play technique through exploration – in this case of painting. It is a pity that most children have to wait three more years before they can move forward from that first magical experience. Not many parents are willing to submit their carpets to the hazard of having paint spilt on them, and so children may not experience the joy of using colour again until they arrive at the playgroup.

Happily they are not deprived of all means of play through graphic expression. Look at fig. 2a. It is redrawn accurately from a scribble by a child of thirteen months. She had reached the stage when she could move rapidly about the house. Her hapless mother had left the magic marker, which she was using to write on the laundry parcel, within the child's reach. Camilla saw the marker, crawled over to it, picked it up, tasted it, tapped with it on the wall and floor. As she tapped she made a sound, she also made a mark. She saw the mark with delight. She made more and bigger marks and sounds by moving the marker backwards and forwards in an automatic motor movement. The result is a typical 'Stage 1' scribble. All children do this at some time with pencil or crayon or whatever is handy. Your child did it. Did you see it happen?

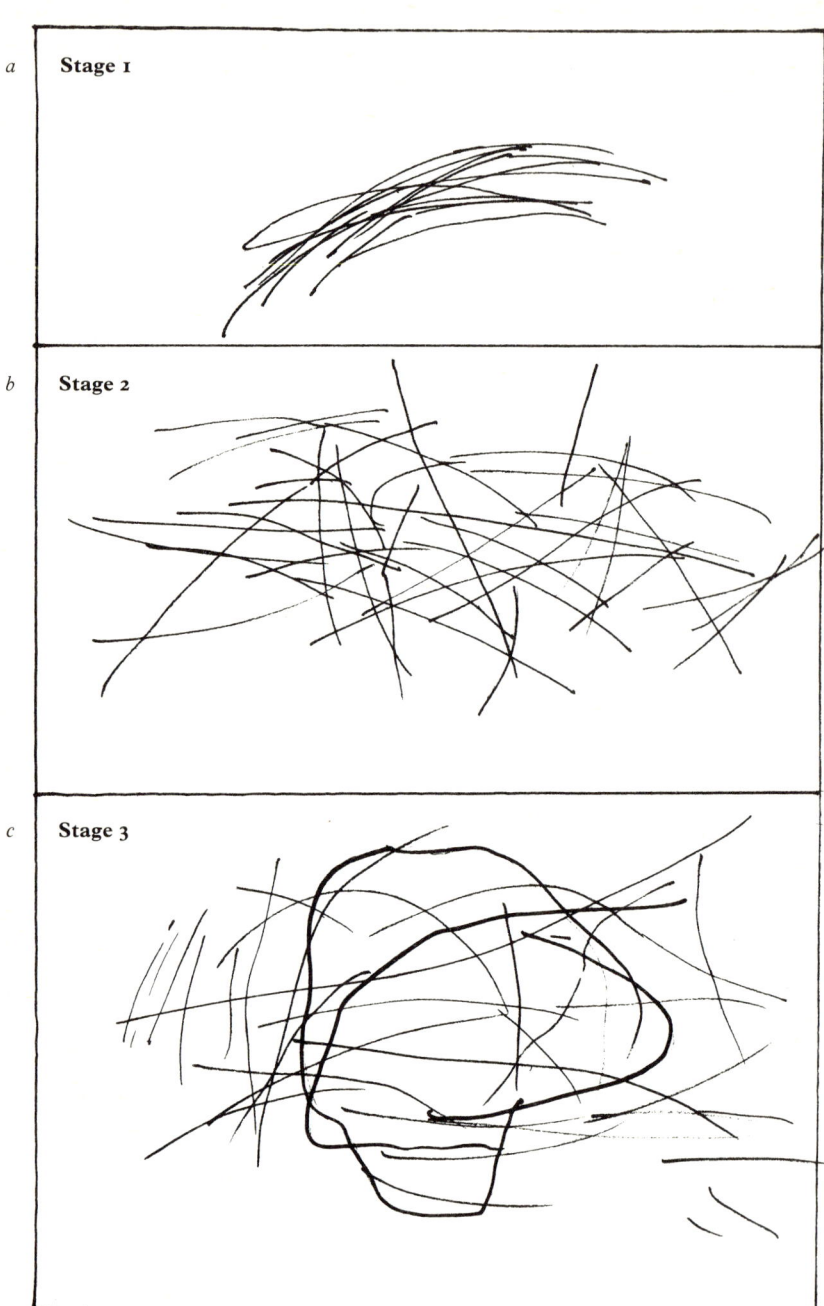

Fig. 2

What does a 'Stage 1' scribble tell us adults about the child who made it? It tells us that, as young as thirteen months, the child has already developed considerable control of arm muscle; and not only muscular control, but also co-ordination between muscles and sight. The child achieves this in graphic terms long before he or she can speak, or think consecutively.

Now compare fig. 2b with fig. 2a. There is a significant difference. Fig. 2a represents a basic and automatic backwards and forwards movement with little variation, with the child listening to the sound of the crayon on the paper and watching the marks appearing. Fig. 2b, a typical 'Stage 2' scribble, is composed of a complex of lines all starting and ending at different points and all travelling in different directions. The eye working together with the arm muscles pre-selected different starting and finishing points. The movement is no longer merely automatic as in fig. 2a. It will readily be realized that infinitely greater muscular control is needed to produce fig. 2b. The 'Stage 2' scribble shows clearly, is evidence, that the child has developed his co-ordination of muscle and sight between the time he produced the 'Stage 1' scribble and when he produced the 'Stage 2' scribble. This is a vital assessment to make in terms of child development.

Fig. 2c shows the next step forward, a 'Stage 3' scribble. The important new feature in this case is the 'round-and-round' line. Once again this implies a significant step forward in control. It usually takes longer to develop than the first two stages. It is a type of scribble, or line work, which the child will produce in paint, crayon, chalk, pencil or other medium in the playgroup. The three stages illustrated plus the ten which follow (fig. 3), all carefully transcribed from the originals, together constitute the universal, instinctual pattern of development in scribble–line–drawing. Examples of these can be observed in any home, any playgroup, any nursery school anywhere in the world. It is a pattern of development which every child finds for himself, without being taught, through a process of play with the marking implement. Research and study show this phenomenon to be common throughout the world in both primitive and advanced cultures alike.

Although it is misleading to give 'ages' (it is more meaningful to talk about 'stages of development'), it is probable that the first scribble will be produced at about twelve months and that stage thirteen would be reached by five years of age.

Fig. 3

Why does the child struggle so hard to develop the skill to produce these primitive symbols? Why does he need them? What does he use them for? Look how this boy, aged four, used his 'Stage 7' (fig. 4). He added three spots to this primitive head and announced, 'It's a boy with chicken pox.'

Fig. 4

Jayne, aged four, was obviously very sad and disturbed when she produced her 'Stage 10' Big-Head figure (fig. 5). After gentle but persistent invitation by the teacher to 'Tell me about your drawing', she finally admitted, distressed and anxious, 'It's a baby girl.' When pressed further on the matter she said, again in a disturbed and emotional state, 'We had a new baby in our house last night.'

Mary, aged four, had reached the stage of being able to make complete figures, 'Stage 13'. Fig. 6a shows how she usually painted herself. Note the way she makes the simplest dots for the eyes. She held a special place in her family because she was the only one who did not wear glasses. Some time later she was found to be suffering from the same eye abnormality as the others. It became necessary for her to wear spectacles and she did not like it at all. In one stroke she had lost her uniqueness. Fig. 6b was the first self-portrait she produced, at playgroup, wearing her glasses. Note the eyes this time. A child of four would find it difficult to put into words her feelings on that occasion; but her drawing is eloquence itself.

Fig. 5

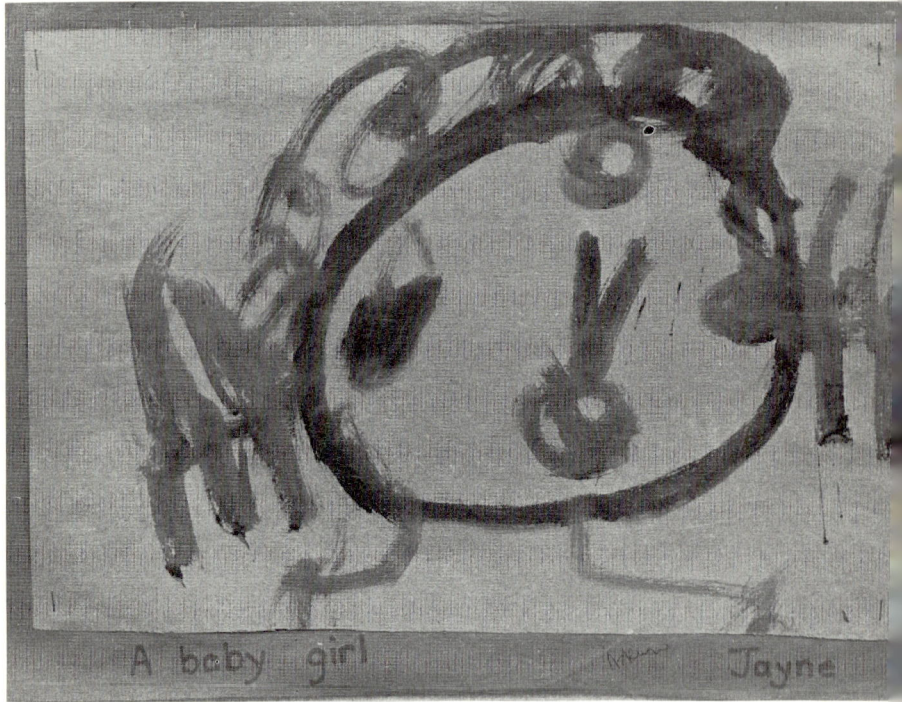

Fig. 6

We can learn much about the child from what he says to, and about, his drawings while and after drawing them.

In the three examples given above the children were using their primitive drawn symbols at three different stages, as Leonard Marsh says in his book *Alongside the Child in the Primary School*,* to relive important experiences. We should remember, when we look at very young children's primitive drawn symbols, that they may contain vital information about their social, and other, experiences.

Perhaps this may be the place to make the point that drawing is basically lines. Much work that is executed in paint and brush consists of line and so is drawing. Figs. 2 and 3 are typical examples. They are linear and so should be thought of as drawings.

All children draw some of the stages.

Some children draw all of the stages.

Some may have completed the drawing sequence long before they begin to attend playgroup or nursery school. Some may race through the whole sequence in two or three weeks after arrival in playgroup or school. Background, intelligence, parental influence all have their effect upon the individual child. The scribble–line sequence illustrated in this book is the norm. Watch out for the various stages. Ask the child if he would like to tell you about his drawing. Do not press him if he does not want to talk. If he does talk you may learn significant information about him from what he says. Do not worry if he fails to respond for the first two or three times.

The child uses his primitive drawn symbols to explain, or state, or re-live experiences which are important to him. We should treat his drawings with respect and think of them as windows through which we can see something of what is going on inside the child's mind.

If the child is allowed to develop his own symbols at his own speed, and if we make ourselves familiar with the scribble–line–drawing pattern of development, then we can assess the child's development, and we can watch him growing up through the various stages of his discoveries.

---

* A. & C. Black, London 1970; Praeger, New York, 1970. This subject is also dealt with in *Pre-School and Infant Art* by Kenneth Jameson, Studio Vista, London, 1968; published in New York as *Art and the Young Child* by Viking, 1969.

Fig. 7

Setting up the drawing situation

There are several ways in which situations can be set up to encourage drawing play. For instance lean a piece of hardboard, say 6 feet by 2 feet (180 cm × 60 cm), rough side out, against the wall with half a dozen chalks nearby, as in fig. 7, or, if funds will run to it, provide a blackboard and/or paper and magic marker, or paints, or crayons.

Be on your guard against reading too much into the children's work. Take what the children say about them at its face value. Forget pseudo-psychological explanations. They are dangerously misleading.

So much for the drawing sequence. Painting, the second of the two sequences, is different in kind. We will now consider it as a separate activity.

The blob–patch–pattern sequence

Painting, as distinct from drawing, is concerned with patches or areas of colour.

It is probably true to say that dabbling with paint is more obviously play than a good many other activities. As an activity it has magical qualities which fascinate virtually all children. A child painting is a child absorbed. Painting provides colour mixing, pattern making, the invocation of fantasy. It has tactile excitement. It provides the child with a situation in which he has the power to 'make' or to 'destroy'. It provides the child with instant, powerful and compelling experience of colour. It imposes the discipline of making choices about colour. It has enormous appeal. Set up the easel in the child's vicinity and in 99 per cent of cases he will be irresistibly drawn to it. The eight examples in fig. 8 show the complete painting sequence, how he starts and how he progresses. 8a and b show two typical first paintings by 'under-fives' who had never used paint before. 8a shows the child tentatively exploring all the available colours by putting blobs all over the paper. 8b, on the other hand, shows the child making a positive choice of *one* colour, in this case blue, and making two big patches all in the same colour. 8b is evidence of a singleminded attitude at the time of painting; 8a shows a child who feels in the mood to explore. 8c reveals much greater competence in fitting the patches of colour together and, in addition, one other important bit of evidence. The large patch was painted red. The child who painted it sought out the red because there was none on the easel when he was ready to start painting. Having found the bright pillar-box red he painted the large area, displaying mouthwatering relish as he did so. Then he neatly fitted the blues, yellows, pinks and the rest round it; but it was the red which stimulated him. He was really excited about it, and this excitement is the next stage after the 'exploring' stage (*a* and *b*). Now he is *expressing* what he feels about a colour (red). He is celebrating red.

8d is the next stage after that. Here the child is making careful choices of different colours which he likes. He then arranges them, organizes them, into a pattern of patches of colour, with great precision. He is only four years old, and nobody showed him how to do it. All young children have an inborn sense of pattern which may show itself in paint, or movement, or music. 8e and 8f are two variants of the painted type, a 'stripe' pattern and a 'flag' pattern both of which will be familiar to playgroup workers, if the children have been allowed to develop spontaneously at their own speed, in their own way and unimpeded by 'help' from adults. 8g is the next stage in the sequence. It is also a patch pattern, with textured enrichment produced by overpainting. 8h shows how the patch pattern painting can very easily be given a touch of realism. The patch colours have been arranged in a 'house' shape with three other shapes making windows. Basically, when she began the work, the little four-year-old girl who produced this was painting a pattern. When she

Fig. 8

had finished it she said, 'A house!' Two days later she made no comment when confronted with the painting. It was not clear whether she recognized her own work. Children do not have much interest in their products except when they are working on them, unless the adult has inculcated within the child the idea that the paintings and the drawings and the other things he has made are important. If the child deduces that the adult considers the work is important – and make no mistake he is sharp enough to be able to deduce it – then this will influence him into thinking the same, whether this is natural to him or not.

It is, however, indisputable that colour, painting and pattern-making give the child exquisite pleasure and vital experience. We must make sure he has access to this exciting activity.

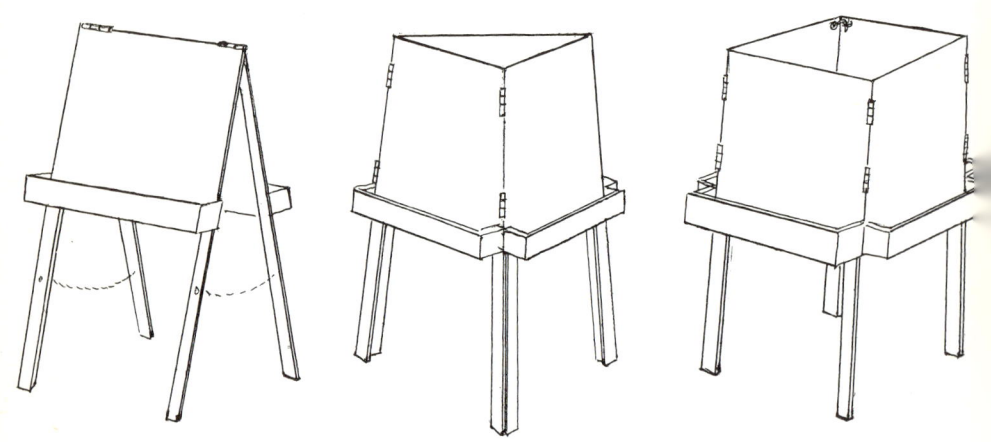

Fig. 9

Setting up the painting situation

The vital factor in providing painting facilities is that they should be always there and that the child should be free to paint whenever he likes. He should be able to paint instantly, the moment he wants to. Children will paint quite happily with their paper on a tarpaulin on the floor, or on a table, or at an easel. Any of these three alternatives is appropriate. Some are easier to organize than others. Without doubt the easiest, the most economical of space, and the best for the child to use is the double-, treble-, or quadruple-sided easel (fig. 9). When using the vertical easel the eye of the child is the same distance from all parts of the painting. Whereas, on a table, especially if it is a bit too tall for the child, the far edge of the work will be much further away than the near edge and as a result it will be harder to reach and the child will have difficulty in seeing the work as it progresses. Easels should have racks and should be self-sufficient with paper clipped on (clothes pegs work well), and pots of ready-mixed paint with a size 10 or 12 round-ferruled hog-hair brush with a long handle in each. Children enjoy using small fine brushes occasionally but these are too fragile for the hurly-burly of most playgroups; they are also expensive. If the easels have no racks then deep trays, of appropriate size to hold say four pots of paint, help to prevent spillages. A four-pint wire or plastic milk carrier is excellent.

It is extremely important that the paint should be on or near the easel. Playgroup children will not paint if they have to ask for brush, paint and paper separately and then have to stand about waiting until the helper provides them. And while we are mentioning inhibiting factors remember that if Mum has said to the child 'Don't you come home with paint on that new frock, or I'll skin you,' *that* too will cause the child to fight shy of painting. If the paint is ready and they are uninhibited the children will paint.

Little children love colour and they are not particular *which* colour. They like it bright, clean and ready for use. Do not be persuaded that it is necessary to provide any special range of colours. So long as you put out three or four, or if possible five, different strong colours the children will be satisfied. If they are not satisfied they will soon let you know which colour is missing! The introduction of primary and secondary colour theory is inappropriate for this age group. For the short time they are in the playgroup or the nursery school just let them enjoy the colour in their own way. There will be time enough for theory later.

When you mix the paints make them not too thick and not too thin. A good test of consistency is to paint a blob on to a vertical paper on an easel. It should not run down. Use this consistency for general purposes. Children also enjoy using 'dribbly' paint, but for normal use a consistency which is just stable on a vertical surface is best.

Paper

Paper is expensive. Get it where you can. Seek out your nearest large firm which uses a computer. They have so much old computer paper, clean on one side, they do not know what to do with it. There are endless supplies of old posters. Your 'local rag' will give you ends of newspaper rolls. Old newspapers can also be used. If you buy papers at local art dealers (i.e. Rowneys, Reeves, Winsor and Newton, and Dryad in the U.K.), ask for brushwork paper or newsprint. These two types are relatively inexpensive. A good deal depends upon what the children are used to. It is best to vary sizes, and shapes if you like, up and down around 22 × 15 inches (55 cm × 40 cm). If it is feasible let the children choose the size and shape they like best.

Brushes

Size 10 or 12 round-ferrule hog-hair brushes are best; but paste brushes from Woolworths, or half-inch house painters brushes will serve. Thin watercolour brushes are not very suitable. The cheap variety wear out in a day and the more durable variety are very expensive. Be on your guard against children sucking brushes; it can be dangerous.

Additives for paint

It is sometimes advocated that detergents or synthetic pastes such as Polycell and other wallpaper pastes should be added to paints as a way of making the supply of paint last longer. The main effect of this is to spoil the innate quality of the paint. The aim of the practice is economy, and financial economy is essential in most playgroups, but it is questionable whether it is wise to eke out the supply of paint if the quality of the painting experience is thereby ruined. These comments apply only to normal painting. Fingerpaint needs to be different in consistency. It is dealt with separately in the following pages.

Drawing and painting are two of the most significant forms of play not least because the record of that play remains afterwards on the paper to be seen and thought about by the adult. Other kinds of play leave no permanent trace – dressing up, dancing. When they are over they vanish. They may never be seen by the adult. Paintings and drawings remain as evidence.

The child advances instinctively through a progression from scribble to line and finally he achieves drawing.

The child develops instinctively through a progression from blob to patch, from patch to pattern and finally achieves painting.

The two sequences are separate and distinct and yet complementary. Remember that the adult's function in both situations is to set it up, to provide the equipment, time and place, and encouragement and then most important of all to stand back and resist the temptation to interfere.

The child who is reluctant to paint

There are very few of these. In cases investigated it has generally turned out that the mother had made threats about likely results if the child marked his clothes with paint. There are other causes but the mother's warnings are the main deterrent. Even the fastidious child finds it difficult to resist the lure of paint. When next you are confronted by a reluctant playgroup painter look elsewhere for the reason than at the easel and the paint pot.

Every child is an individual and as such will have individual tastes and interests. He will want to try everything in the playgroup in turn, when *he* wants to, and that may not be when *you* want him to. If he shows reluctance it is likely to be only temporary.

In the very rare case of the genuinely reluctant painter do not press him too hard. Make sure he is 'accidentally' confronted with the easel and paint from time to time, but if he still avoids it do not worry, so long as he is normal in other respects. It is not a disaster if he delays his acquaintance with paint until he reaches infant school or kindergarten. The chances are he will find satisfaction and expression, in dressing up, climbing, running, jumping, dancing, singing, shouting, building, etc.

Mother's natural disquiet about soiled clothes can be abated by insisting that all the children wear aprons or some other kind of protective clothing for painting. A word in season with her before junior arrives in playgroup may well avoid the damaged clothes difficulty. See page 101, 'Practicalities', for suggestions for pinafores, etc.

N.B. The scribble – line – drawings in figs. 2 and 3 and the paintings in fig. 8 are scrupulously careful copies of actual children's work.

Finger-painting

Finger painting is closely linked with the earlier dabbling with food. It is playing with paint. It is a visual, physical and tactile activity in which the child experiences the pleasures of sense of touch, the visual excitement of watching swirling patterns trailing after his finger tips and the exhilaration of vigorous arm movements as well as the fascination of making minute marks and touches.

Setting up the finger-painting situation

When setting up the finger-painting for the first time all you need do is provide a pool of suitable paint directly on, if possible, a formica or other plastic or lino table top. An egg-cupful will do to start with. Just pour the paint on and do nothing more. Some of the children will be bound to see you pouring. When you have placed the paint move a little distance away and watch. It will not be long before some will be dabbling, first fingers, then hands, first tentatively and then enthusiastically. They will not need to be shown how to spread or how to manipulate, to watch the effects they themselves are making, to enjoy and to swim in the paint. Watch without interfering and you will see them both paint, by spreading flat areas, and draw with the tip of the finger in the spread paint. When they have finished they should be encouraged to sponge off the table top ready for the next participant.

A suitable recipe for making finger-paint is to prepare smoothly mixed cold water paste and add powder colour to give the consistency of cream. Alternatively, if funds will run to it, prepared finger-paint is obtainable from artists' suppliers. A second home-made recipe is to use good quality washing-up liquid instead of the cold water paste when using the powder form of colour. Most brands of dry powder colour and ready mixed finger-paint are non-toxic but it is always as well to double check when ordering. Another method of working is to pour the liquid paste on to the table top and allow the child to add dry powder paint. This is sometimes wasteful because the child does not know when enough is enough. Also, putting too much powder into the paste makes the consistency too dry and work will be difficult. However, a useful limitation can be achieved by supplying a small lollipop stick to ladle out the paint.

Finger-painting on paper is not very satisfactory. The size of the paper can be a limiting factor. If the paper is too absorbent the paint will dry out and work will be impossible. If it is too thin and too wet it will tear. It may slip on a smooth table top. All in all liquid paint on a smooth non-absorbent table top is best (fig. 10). But try all methods and see which best pleases the child. What is important is that it should be a fluent vigorous activity. The effects are short-lived. Treat them as such. The child does. A child of three years would never think of taking prints from his finger-painting patterns though this adult ploy is sometimes imposed on the children. Resist this tendency even under the pretext of 'keeping a record' of the work. If you show the child how to perform a trick of this kind you may find that it is the thin end of a very dubious wedge, and the child may look to you for other tricks to perform.

Fig. 10

Clay, play-dough, plasticine

Do not think of these three as modelling materials. If you do you will tend to expect 'results' rather than 'experiences'. If the children produce 'big-head' figures (see fig. 5) – dogs, birds and the rest – well and good but these should be considered as by-products. Give a child a piece of malleable material and watch what happens. He will delight in banging it on the table, flattening it, squeezing it, pressing it and in other ways imposing his will upon it by manipulation. This is the real value of providing plastic material for the child. It provides him with a means of coming to terms with an agency outside himself. Camilla, aged two and a half, when presented with a ball of clay, proceeded to break up the clay into small pieces about as big as a sugar-lump. She then arranged these in neat rows and continued until all of the large lump was divided.

Daren, aged three, had been at playgroup for six weeks. He had played enthusiastically all morning, mostly with sand and water. While the children were listening to a story a mother put several large lumps of clay on a low table. Released from story time Daren made straight for the clay and immediately began punching rhythmically, first with one hand then with the other half singing to himself 'Bash! Bash! – Bash! Bash!' He then picked it up and dropped it on the table, looking rather surprised that it flattened itself out a little. He poked it gently with his finger and then pushed his finger in as far as it would go. He then withdrew his finger and examined the hole. All this time he was completely engrossed with his clay activity. At this point a playleader put some rolling pins on the table. Daren picked one up, looked at the other children, rolled the clay once or twice, in an offhand manner, hit his neighbour lightly on the head with the rolling pin and then wandered off, looking rather aimlessly round the room. Had the coming of the rolling pin helped or hindered his play?

The two examples given above indicate that the child has his own ideas about what he likes to do. As it happens they were both examples of clay. The same applies to all three of the materials included under this present heading. Clay, dough, and plasticine have some characteristics in common and some important differences. The dissimilarities are significant enough to need a separate paragraph on each.

Clay

Clay is supplied in two general types: terra cotta, which is red; and buff or grey. The most important characteristic of clay, for the child to play with, or for the artist to work with, is the degree to which it can be poked, bent, pulled, twisted, stretched, squeezed, and moulded, in other words its plasticity.

The plasticity of the clay is proportionate to the amount of water it contains. If it is too wet it will stick to hands, table top and everything else. If it is too dry it will be too hard to manage. At the end of a morning session in hot small hands clay will have lost a great deal of its necessary moisture and this will have to be put back if the clay is to be used again. The value of clay at home and in the playgroup depends upon there being a helper who is sufficiently knowledgeable to keep the clay in workable condition. Simple rules for this are as follows:

(1) Buy clay ready for use and choose a source of supply that sells it in airtight polythene sacks.
(2) Store it in a small dustbin or breadbin, or in large tins with close-fitting lids.
(3) Include a wet cloth in each container to keep the air inside damp.
(4) Keep a second tin for dried clay and when it is two thirds full pour water in and let it soak for at least 24 hours. When it can be handled, i.e. when the clay has absorbed the water, take out a handful, roll it into a ten-inch sausage. Double it into two and roll it out until it is ten inches long again. Repeat this many times until the clay is of even consistency all through. It is then ready for re-use. The process is not so long-winded as it sounds.

There are various proprietary clays on the market but simple potters' clay is best and cheapest.

Do not expect any particular kind of results. The activity, the play and the resultant experiences are what matter. Slapping, slopping, poking, pushing, stroking, dividing into small bits, and arranging the bits, are the likely activities. Unrecognizable bitty shapes will be 'imagined' into birds, men, fire engines, jet planes. That they look to the adult nothing like any of these things is likely but immaterial. What the child *says* it is, it *is*, to the child; and the child is the chief consideration in this case.

The main advantage of clay, compared with dough and plasticine, is that it provides perhaps the most exciting and expressive play experience of any of the three-dimensional media. Its main disadvantage is that it is messy; the wetter the messier! There is a limit to the hall caretaker's patience. Clay treads about and marks clothes. Aprons and tarpaulin can be effective.

Set up clay play by providing a low table 4 feet by 4 feet (1·20 m × 1·20 m), or two tables 4 feet by 2 feet (1·20 m × 60 cm) side by side. Place a main, largish lump of clay in the centre of the table and, say, four balls of clay, about the size of a tennis ball, one on each side of the table. Put out, at the beginning, one or two small wooden modelling tools. Stand back and observe.

Play-dough

Children enjoy using dough and it has become a staple material in playgroups. It is also gaining popularity for younger children at home. Many of the experiences described above in clay can be gained from dough. Dough can be bought from artists' shops but it is much cheaper to make it at home.

Recipe

Use plain flour. Add cold water slowly and knead it, keeping even wetness throughout. Avoid too much water or you will end up with a sticky unmanageable mass. A small addition of salt will act as a short-term preservative; not too much or it will render the mixture too short. Add a little powder paint if you wish to colour it.

Advantages of play-dough: it can be made from readily available materials. It is relatively clean. Colour can be varied. It is cheap to make.

Disadvantages of play-dough: it is less plastic than clay. Dough pieces cannot be joined together as easily as clay pieces can. It is slightly elastic in texture and this makes it less obedient in the hands of the user.

Set up the play-dough table in the same way as the clay table.

Plasticine

Plasticine is an old stand-by and is popular with children. It can be obtained in convenient one-pound packs, and is produced in attractive colours. It is most suitable for small-scale work. It is a 'dry' material which remains pliable, though it will harden to some extent if left in the open air, but it is not so malleable for small fingers as natural clay in good working condition. Accordingly it is not a satisfactory substitute for clay or play-dough. By itself it would not provide adequate three-dimensional touch experience but, as an extra, if you have a stock of plasticine, by all means let the children use it.

Tools

Keep a few pastry cutters or tin lids handy and use these some days but not always (fig. 11). Also provide a few modelling sticks (lollipop sticks will do) or any other accessories you can think of which will stab, cut or shape clay. One broom handle cut into 12-inch lengths will make four or five rolling pins.

Let the children work on the table top. Modelling boards slip and move about and are more trouble than they are worth.

Keep an eye on children who show a tendency to eat clay, or dough, or plasticine.

When providing tools put them out before the children start the activity.

Fig. 11

Costs

There is a big difference in cost between the five main modelling materials. In order of price they are: clay collected by the buyer, from the producer, in bulk; clay bought in smaller quantities from art stores; home-made play-dough; plasticine from art stores; play-dough bought from art stores. Clay from the producer is the least expensive, play-dough the dearest. The diagram below is worked out mathematically to scale from current prices. The black bands show variations in quantity of modelling material you could expect to receive if the same amount of money were spent on each type.

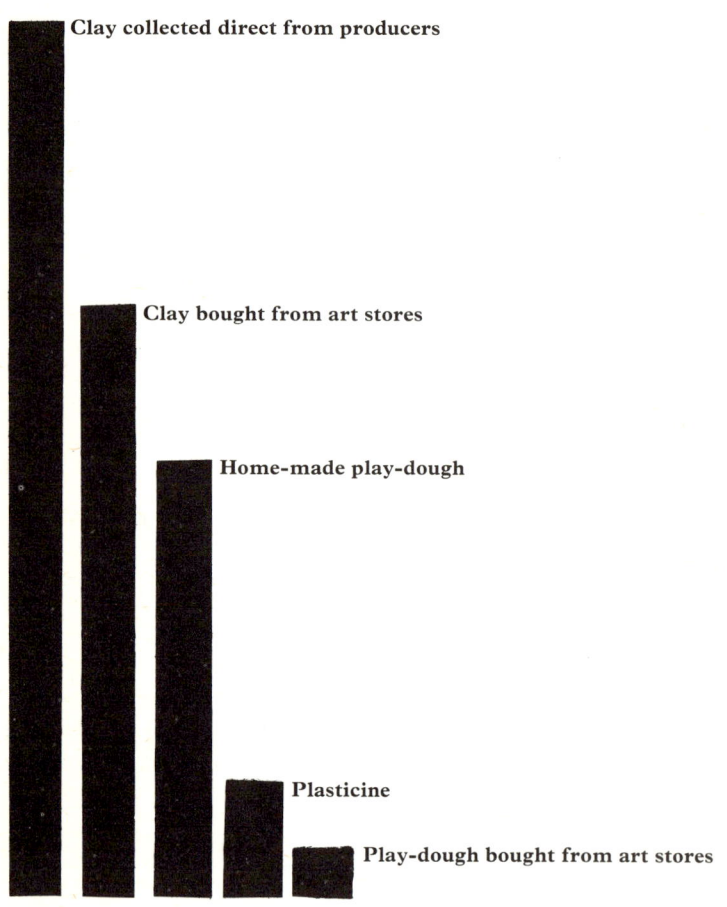

Clay collected direct from producers

Clay bought from art stores

Home-made play-dough

Plasticine

Play-dough bought from art stores

Fig. 12

Woodwork

Provide if possible a low-level bench (fig. 12) with a vice or clamp, to secure wood which is being hammered or sawn. If no bench is available try to provide an old wooden-top table cut to the appropriate height.

Toy tools are a waste of money and frustrating for the children. Toy saws bend too much and toy hammers are too small to be effective. Provide small-size 'real' tools and some $1\frac{1}{2}$ and 2 inch nails (4 cm × 5 cm). The grocer, greengrocer, the nearby building site, the woodwork shop in the local secondary school, the timber yard, can be coaxed to part with off-cuts and empty wooden boxes.

The basic tool kit should include a small tenon saw with a slim handle, a 4 oz hammer (125 gm), pincers and glass-paper blocks. Buy the best hammer you can afford as a cheap one may have a 'soft' face and quickly become marked. Look after saws carefully. Sharp saws cut through wood but blunt ones may slip and cut fingers.

At a later stage, add a small hand-drill, a screwdriver with a short sturdy blade and fat handle, and a few screws.

If tools are well looked after and the wood not too hard there need be no fear of accidents. The children become so absorbed in what they are doing that they have no time to misuse the tools. The bench space allows only two or three children to participate at one time and so the activity is easy to supervise.

It is unlikely that any masterpieces of the cabinet-maker's art will be produced but the boys – and girls – will give vent to their enthusiasms by banging and sawing.

Educational Supply Association Ltd and possibly other local education suppliers supply a woodwork bench that is suitable for three- to five-year-olds and is not too expensive.

Printing table

It is only too easy to fall into the error of showing pre-school children how to make things and how to do things, a process a little better than teaching them how to perform tricks. It is an error because as soon as the adult begins to demonstrate he becomes a performer in the eyes of the child, a kind of conjurer. Children of all ages have an insatiable appetite for this kind of show, and the young ones are no exception. They also have a keen desire to imitate. They learn by imitation, but it must be remembered that the value of the exercise lies in imitation of the activity of the adult, not of the work of art the adult produces. If the adult produces a complicated or sophisticated work of art the child attempting to imitate it will fail to copy it successfully and will become frustrated. If once the child is led to believe that the adult knows best he will adopt the adult's model and will abandon his own. In other words he will become dependent upon the adult, and we know to our cost the effect of dependence. Our aim should be to help the child to trust himself and to become independent. For this reason we must put him into situations where he can explore and find, for himself, independent of the adult. This applies particularly to children who are by nature somewhat dependent emotionally and psychologically. The printing table in unwary hands can open the way to 'trick teaching', so think first. Printing should be offered in its simplest form.

Setting up the printing table

An opportunity for the child to explore and find is provided by means of a printing table (fig. 13). You need a low table top about 4 feet by 4 feet (120 cm × 120 cm) or two narrower tables set side by side will serve. Take a large tin lid, any shape will do. Cut a piece of foam rubber half an inch thick and fit it into the lid. Soak the foam rubber with dark coloured fluid paint – ink if you dare! – and place it in the centre of the table. Find as many suitable objects as you can, corks, woodblocks, matchbox covers, cotton reels, balls of screwed-up paper, and range them round the tin-lid ink-pad in the middle of the table. Place pieces of paper round the working surface of the table. Do not demonstrate anything, just watch the children. It will not be long before someone will be attracted to the scene, will dip his finger in the inky pad, will then press his finger on the table top, or paper, and will leave a finger print behind, and will see that he has done so. Then a more venturesome hand will join in. The activity will be catching and will lead naturally to using the printing blocks, cotton reels, woodblocks, corks and the rest. If the play-group policy is to use this approach throughout the children will invent and find out by themselves led on by their inborn curiosity and their tendency to 'get into things'. This is the creative way. The uncreative way is for the child to be asked to copy the adult. Sadly too many adult-inspired leafprints are still to be seen; too many folded-blob patterns; too many prints of finger-paintings. Children exposed to the above type of activity will develop the attitude, 'I wonder what she will show us today'. They will wait for the initiative to come from the playleader when in fact they would otherwise be taking the initiative themselves.

Fig. 13

Experimenting with junk

Provide as many different varieties of boxes, packing, containers, dispensers and cardboard tubes as you can find. Virtually all commodities these days are distributed in packages of one kind or another. The result is a profusion of re-usable junk which is available at no cost. Provide also a good strong adhesive. Marvin Medium, Rowney's P.V.A. Medium, Gloy Multiglue, Elmer's, etc. are all powerful stickers which children can use safely.

The title above avoids the term junk-modelling deliberately because the use of it would seem to imply that a model is to be made with junk. Having provided the raw materials, just stand back and let the children play with the materials (fig. 14). Try the experiment of supplying all the items suggested above and withdraw to a distance and watch. If amongst the junk there is a

Fig. 14

large round cardboard lid, or a tin lid, the chances are a thousand to one that a child will pick it up and steer his way round the room using it as a steering wheel to the accompaniment of motor car noises. If there is a suitable sized shoe box it will not be long before it is used as a bed for the doll.

As for the constructors, the mechanics, the imaginative children, they will need no prompting to join things together to make things. They will, however, benefit if they are shown how adhesive works. A technical tip of this kind helps and is valid, but let the adult's intervention stop there. If the play-leader is tempted to go further and show the child how to make a light-house out of a toilet-roll middle the effect will be self-defeating. We do not want to see how well a child can copy the adult. We want to release the individual inventiveness of each child. If we cause him to imitate we put him in a straitjacket and prevent the free flow of his own imagination, and he may become dependent upon the adult for a lead every time.

Collage and sticky table

Children greatly enjoy using sticky tape and glue. They regard the fact that Selotape (Scotch tape) adheres to other substances, and that paper can be glued to paper, as a kind of magic. The fun of sticking is what they enjoy (fig. 15). The word collage is somewhat over-impressive, used in this context, for the natural and simple childish activity of 'collecting'. You cannot have escaped watching and hearing a little girl saying, 'I'll have a bit of that,' (gold lamé). 'Look at these!' (sequins). 'It's soft,' (red velvet). She collects all these and sticks them to *her* paper. It then becomes her own special collection, personal to that child. The collecting and the visual and tactile experiences resulting from the collecting are what matter. The resulting 'work of art' is unimportant, or at least, of secondary importance (fig. 16). The sticking, and massing together, the seeing, the choosing, and loving the attractive bits are the vital activities, a primitive technique of sticking, allied to two aesthetic activities, visual selection and pattern-making, constitute the value of the sticky table.

Fig. 15

Fig. 16

Setting up the sticky table is simplicity itself. Place a box of pretty bits, a pot of strong adhesive such as Elmer's, Marvin Medium, Rowney's P.V.A. or Gloy Multiglue, and some pieces of paper on the table and stand back and observe.

Remember:
(1) Frequently to replace and/or replenish the bits in the box. Dirty bits are unhygienic and unattractive.
(2) That Selotape (Scotch tape) is expensive and it is also somewhat tricky for small fingers to manage and probably beyond their strength to break, so serve it cut into 3-inch lengths (1·5 cm wide) and stuck round the edge of a dinner plate.

Taking work home

An interesting experiment was carried out in one playgroup. The mothers were asked to help by not suggesting to children that they should bring work home. The playgroup helpers also adopted the same attitude and agreed not to suggest to the children that they might like to take their work back to their parents. As a result the children did not show any desire to take their paintings home, nor even suggest it. There are two important inferences to be drawn from this. First, unless an adult suggests it the child will not normally, of his own volition, want to take work, more especially paintings, home. Second, the child is interested in his work while he is producing it. The interest quickly fades afterwards.

Try a test. Collect all the paintings produced in one day. Dry them, put them away and, a week later, go through them with the children and check how many will identify their own work.

If parents understand that what may appear to be meaningless and often messy blobs are in fact very meaningful to the child at the moment they are done, if the parent is prepared to respect and be interested in the child's work, then no harm will arise when work is taken home. But children, even as young as three or four, can be hurt. 'Not another of those daubs', 'Throw it away', can be a shattering blow to the child's enthusiasm. As Rhoda Kellogg, an American pioneer of child art, says, 'If you throw a child's work into the dustbin a little of the child goes into the bin with it.'

It is necessary to help all the mothers to understand that there is great significance in the children's work – all the work, such as drawings, painting, junk work, and woodwork. Until they do it may be better to keep the work in the playgroup. Make a start by talking to them when they come to fetch their offspring at the end of the daily session. Talk about the work on the drying line or on display on the wall.

Display

If you are lucky enough to have accommodation where you can leave pictures on display make sure the display is carried out to a minimum standard. Let it be tidy. Pin down all the corners. Make sure you include examples of all the work by the children whatever you privately and personally think about the pictures. Try to avoid setting trends. If you do the children will very quickly get to know what you like and may begin to paint so as to get a picture on the wall, in other words painting what you like rather than what they want to.

Sometimes special displays seem appropriate. Christmas is such a time, so let us discuss this as a special case.

Christmas decorations and display

Christmas is, or should be, a happy time, especially for young children. Adults expend energy and thought upon ways of celebrating the festival. One aspect of making merry is to create a visually exciting interior, by decorating the home, the playgroup, the classroom. This is proper to the season, but be on your guard. Do not fall into the trap of showing the children how to make fluffy Father Christmasses and clichéd triangular Christmas trees, and jolly robins. Avoid using the children as spare labour to help with the Christmas frieze which, invariably, is adult-inspired, -organized and -controlled. It is a meaningless activity for the child. Better by far to make a celebration display of their normal work re-inforced perhaps by evergreens, tinsel and glittery glass balls and paper decorations. One procedure is for the adults to send the children home and decorate the room themselves, using perhaps colourful collages made by the children at the sticky table with Christmassy material; glitter, gold ribbon, polystyrene bobbles, metallic papers and bright bits and pieces. The impact upon the children will be all the greater if they walk unexpectedly into a new Christmas world instead of their usual playroom.

Christmas decorations are an adult convention. If children are involved as little as possible in their making, they can experience the joy and exhilaration of walking into a magically changed environment. Can't you recapture the magic of such a moment when you think back to childhood?

Cooking

It is probably true to say that cooking is more a craft than a creative activity. That is to say, the end product is more important as children like to be able to eat the results of their play.

Cooking is of particular interest to the older children and is enjoyed by boys and girls alike. Four to six children can take part at one time but each should have his own bowl and mixing spoon (fig. 17). This is much more satisfying than when all join in stirring a communal mix.

Fig. 17

Toby was a member of a group who made himself unpopular because he would settle to nothing. His sole desire seemed to be to wreck the other children's play. One morning cooking was provided and much to everyone's surprise Toby washed his hands, donned his apron and began to take part. All the ingredients were put into one big bowl and while the measuring-out was being done by the children Toby watched, engrossed. He was allowed to stir the mixture first. But then he had to wait while four other children had their turn. The delay was too much for him. He flung off his apron and dashed to the sand tray where he knocked down the other children's sand and began to throw it about.

Toby's reaction was not exceptional. Children become completely involved in cooking but for this to happen they need to have their own bowl and to see the process through from beginning to end.

The playleader should have the utensils, plus the required ingredients, set out on the tables before the 'cooks' arrive. The activity should begin with hand-washing and putting on aprons. It ends when the last washing-up is done. Children enjoy the clearing-up as much as the activity itself, if it is presented as one part of a total process. It is the adult who finds the washing-up a bore!

If the mixture is to be cooked the children should at least see it placed in the oven. They should be present when the door is opened and the results taken out. Some playleaders allow a child to light the oven, under careful supervision. A great deal about the need to take care with hot things may be learned in this situation. If you are too worried to do this then prepare the oven yourself while the children watch.

The absence of an oven does not mean that cooking has to be avoided. Many groups have successfully iced and decorated biscuits, made peppermint creams, or simply made sandwiches, sometimes from the mustard and cress grown on the playgroup shelf.

Some useful recipes may be found in *Floury Fingers* by Cecilia H. Hinde.* Among the tried and tested examples are rock cakes, cherry cakes, coconut buns, chocolate crispies, jam tarts and currant biscuits.

---

* Faber & Faber, London; Transatlantic Arts Inc., Levittown, New York.

Magic

Virtually every activity in which the child engages contains an element of magic. With paint one can change a white paper into a blue paper. That is magic. A blob of glue makes two pieces of card stick together. That is magic. Hold a piece of red transparent plastic close to the eye, look through, and the world is magically changed to red. A paper crown, however primitive, transports the child to a make-believe world of palaces and princes. The whispery touch of sand particles on the skin, the cold shock of a glittering cascade of water, all are magic. The adult has experienced them all before but to the three-year-old they are new, first time, and magical. Water holds an inescapable attraction for young children. It has magic of many kinds, for the eye, the touch; it splashes, audibly, it pours, sprinkles, drips. Let the young child play with water in the safe situation of the playgroup.

Water play

Water play is a popular and absorbing activity both in the home and in the playgroup. It is not necessarily expensive to equip. A baby bath will do if funds are short though it is not really big enough for exciting water play. If you can acquire an old-fashioned galvanized bath this will serve very well; but if none is available try to afford a container at least 30 inches by 20 inches by 10 inches (70 cm × 50 cm × 25 cm) on a stand 22 inches (55 cm) high, see fig. 18. Provide an additional separate container – a large plastic bowl is ideal – for the water play equipment so that the water in the main container is not 'lost' under a mass of toys. Plastic ducks and boats are suitable for bathtime at home, but they are hardly worth the space they take up in playgroup. The enchantment for the child is to enjoy the 'wateriness' of the water, of filling, pouring, making fountains, seeing the diamond sparkling drops, feeling the wetness, listening to the lapping and the plopping and the splashing.

Small equipment should include plastic jugs, funnels, tubing of different diameters, a sieve, various sizes of pots, a toy teapot, or small indoor-plant watering-can. There should also be containers which look alike but have holes of varying sizes in various places. These can be made from washing-up liquid bottles of the plastic type with their caps cut off. There should be, for instance, one with small holes in the side only, one with small holes in the base only, and as many variations on this theme as you can think of. A good way of making the holes is to push one end of a knitting needle into a largish cork. Use the cork as a handle. Heat the other end of the knitting needle and use the hot end to make holes in the plastic as required. It improves the appearance of the water-play toys if they are given a coat of paint.

Several small absorbent cloths should be kept handy, plus a bucket, for mopping up spillages. If the children are encouraged to clean up by themselves, from the start, it soon becomes automatic and takes its place as part of their play.

By providing a good variety of equipment you cater for children at all stages of development, from those who simply want to pour and fill and feel the water, to those who will be saying to themselves, 'Why does the water come out of this bottle more slowly than from that one?' or, 'Why can't I keep the water in the sieve?'

A useful addition to the equipment suggested above is a collection of objects which float and a collection which sink. Hold a cork below the surface. Release it and it will shoot up again. That is magic.

It is important to provide a wide variety of equipment but remember not to put out every single thing every day because many children become confused by being presented with too much at one time. Interest will be sustained over longer periods of the term if the children find different things provided from time to time.

The sensitive adult will learn to judge just the right moment to step in and encourage the older child, through conversation, to further experiment, and when to stand back and simply let the child take delight in the magic of what he is doing.

Fig. 18

Fig. 19

Bubbles

What could be more magical, to adult and child alike, than soap bubbles floating through the air, iridescent, fragile (fig. 19). Fashions change, the old clay bubble pipes have given way to metal rings or tubes, but the magic is the same. Keep an outfit handy.

Fig. 20

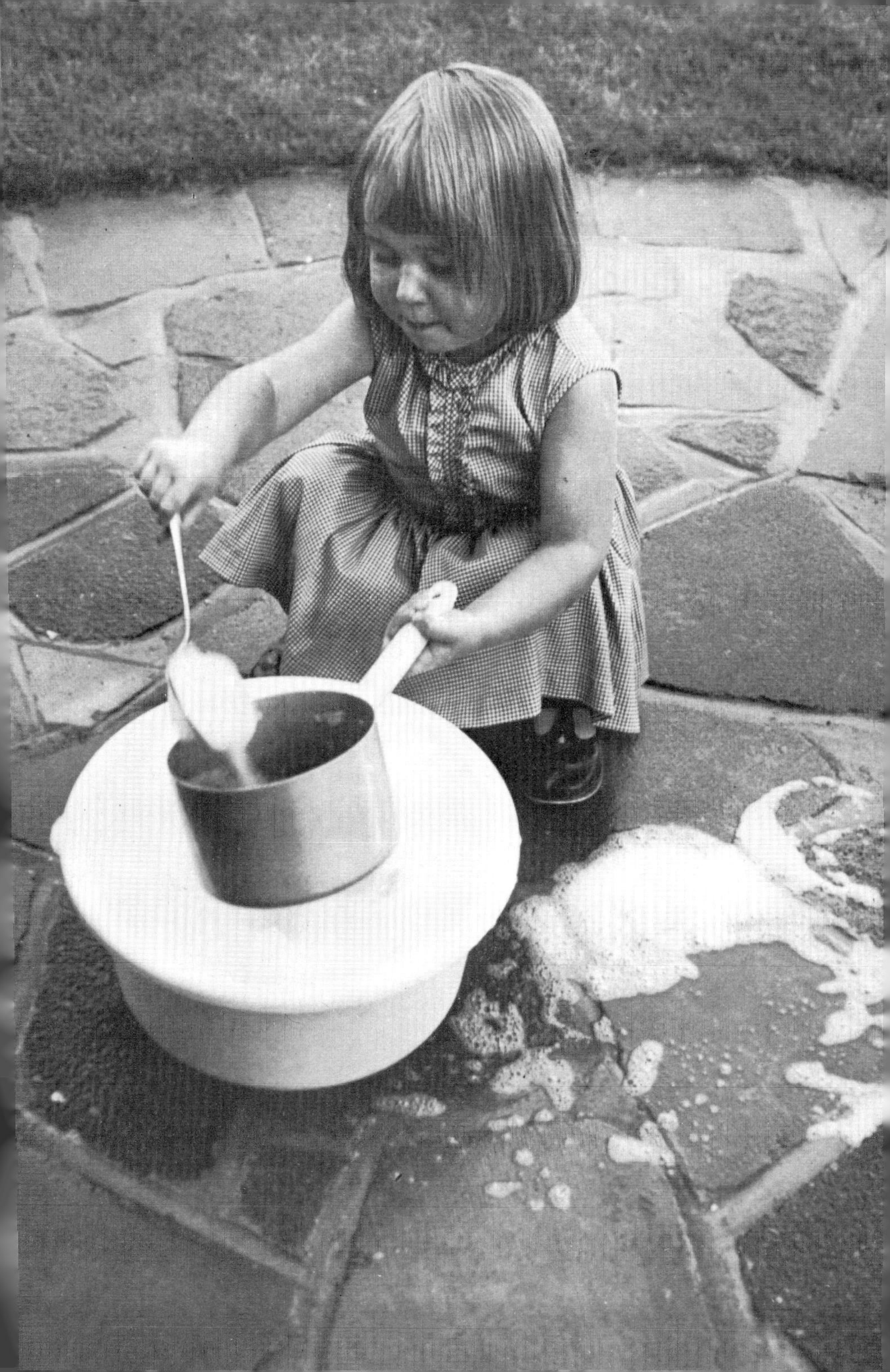

Bubble bowl

A washing-up bowl with warm water and a good squirt of detergent will provide a three-inch layer of bubbly foam (fig. 20). Camilla, aged 2 years 8 months, was standing on a stool 'helping' with the washing-up. She delicately touched the surface of the glistening suds, listened as they whispered and popped. She scooped up handfuls of the foam, filled a cup, transferred it to a small saucepan, squeezed it, poured it. The adult washer-up withdrew and Camilla continued playing absorbed, for nearly half an hour. How many of us adults find magic in washing-up? If the child finds it let him enjoy it. Childhood is short. Let the child enjoy the moment while he has it. Magic for most of us is in short supply. Let us not deny it to the children.

Fig. 21

Sand play

Sand is, for young children, a versatile and evocative medium and its usefulness as a play material can be doubled if two trays are supplied, one with wet sand and one with dry.

A suitable container is necessary. It should be in the form of a large deep tray. Metal, plastic, enamel or wood will serve and where funds are short many improvisations are possible. The important factors are the dimensions of the container and the working height of it. Local educational suppliers, such as Educational Supply Association Ltd, supply an ideal, adaptable version which can be used for both types of sand and for water play. The top should measure about 22 inches by 42 inches by 6 inches (55 cm × 105 cm × 15 cm) and it should stand on wooden legs, one pair with castors, 24 inches high (60 cm). These are ideal dimensions. Fig. 21 gives an indication of the commercial article and fig. 22 shows an improvised table for dry sand made from a sheet of hardboard and 6 inches by 1 inch (15 cm × 2·5 cm) planed softwood. Fig. 23 shows the tray in use.

Dry sand

Put out a sand tray with a heap of dry sand in the middle and watch what happens. Silver sand is best. Ordinary builders' sand will stain clothes and hands. The children will spread the sand, they will heap it, they will pat it, poke it, draw their fingers through it making a pattern of lines, and they will carefully obliterate the lines by smoothing the surface flat. They will press holes and dents with bricks and other 'tools'. Keep a box of accessories *under* the sand tray. They will take handfuls of sand and let it trickle and feel it tickling their skin. They will pour it from containers, through funnels, just like water. They will discover that dry sand does not make sand pies.

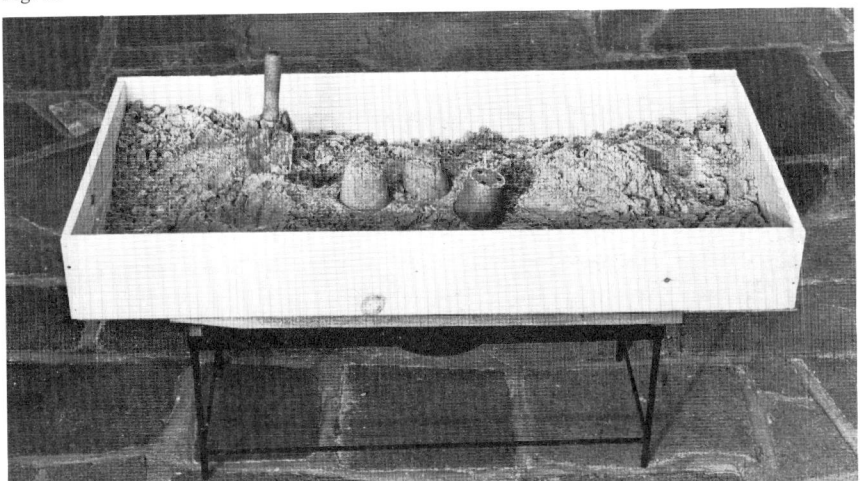

Fig. 22

Fig. 23

Wet sand

For wet sand use washed plastering sand, obtainable from builders' merchants. Unwashed sand will stain clothes and hands and will irritate mothers.

Wet sand is virtually a different substance from dry sand. Its main difference is that it is now sticky and can be made into piles, balls, sand castles, walls, holes, tunnels, imaginary roads, garages, mountains and indeed anything the child's vivid imagination invents. The wet sand is not a modelling medium. It is a generator of play fantasy. Children will happily combine in groups of twos and threes to produce highly intricate structures and to engage in elaborate games with both wet and dry sand.

Provide some tools, i.e. small buckets, trowels, spoons, but not too many, and, as suggested above, keep them under the sand tray. The sand itself is the important experience. Do not smother it with too many accessories. Keep a dustpan and brush handy.

Caution

It is very important to restrain the children from throwing sand about. It is painful if it gets into the eyes and is also dangerous. If you have the use of adjacent play space outside consider building a sand pit. Make sure you provide it with a wire netting cover to discourage marauding cats at night!

Building

Building blocks and building bricks

Play situations divide into two broad categories, group play involving two, three, or four, or more, children playing together; and individual play in which the child plays alone and privately. The large type of building blocks provide the basis for both types but offer greater incentives for group play. For instance, rows of large blocks ranged one behind another make a bus. A bus needs several helpers to build it. When it is made it needs a driver, a conductor, a man to mend it and also an inspector. Small building bricks as distinct from the large building blocks (see fig. 25) also provide stimulus for both group and individual play but are best used by a child in a solitary way, communicating with himself, on half a table, or in a corner of a room on the floor (fig. 24).

In most aspects of play certain basic equipment is necessary. It need not be expensive, but it must be adequate. Little children enjoy colourful, new, shiny apparatus but imaginative play prompted by quite primitive playthings is just as vivid and just as beneficial to the child as play with expensive products.

Fig. 24

Fig. 25

Fig. 26

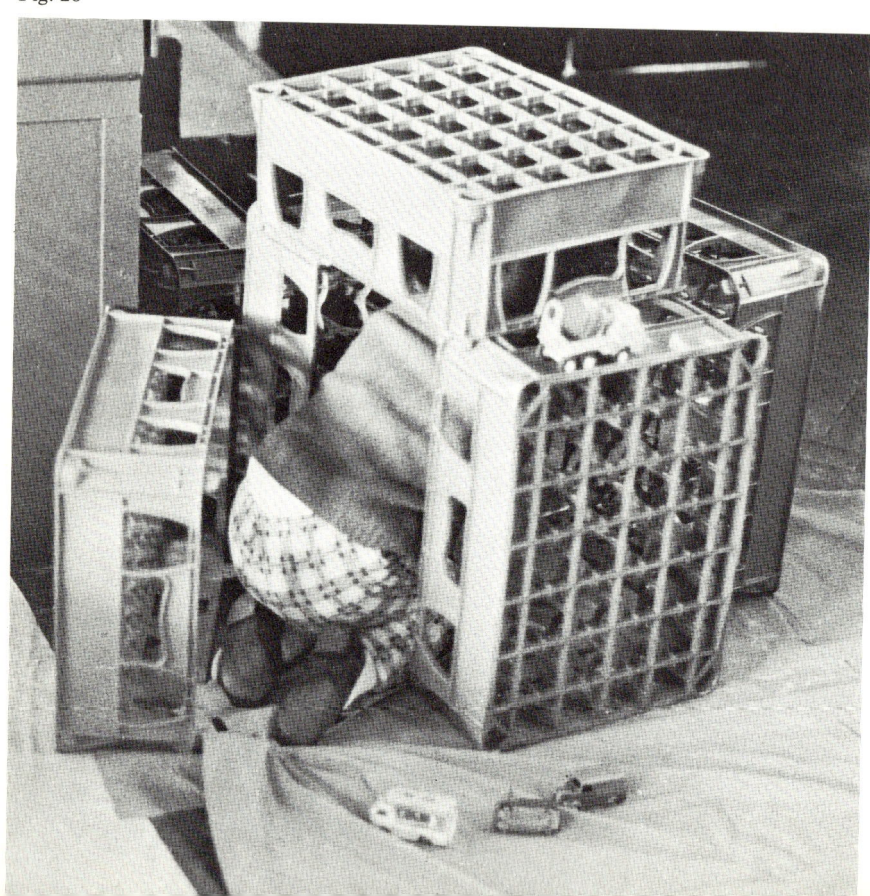

Fig. 25 shows a mixture of building blocks and bricks. At the bottom are building bricks of uniform size made by cutting $3\frac{1}{2}$-inch (9 cm) lengths from a strip of $1\frac{1}{2}$ by 1 inch (4 cm × 2·5 cm) planed softwood. If possible provide a large sackful, in other words several hundreds, all the same size. Next to them in the illustration is an assortment of offcuts collected from building sites, carpenters' shops, secondary-school woodwork shops, timber yards, sawmills. Above are building blocks made by playgroup fathers from hardboard and wood 12 inches by 7 inches by 6 inches (30 cm × 18 cm × 15 cm). To the right of those are the commercial variety, and the remaining small group shows grocers' cartons encased in pasted paper. These serve as lightweight large-scale building blocks at virtually no cost.

Improvised building materials

Milk bottle crates are imaginatively used in the playgroup in fig. 26. Six were presented to the children by the local dairy. In the illustration the children are playing at 'zoos'. The crates are bright red in colour and made from smooth plastic material. There is no danger from sharp edges and they are tough enough to stand rough use. Mark, aged three and a half, spent nearly forty minutes piling one crate on top of another to make a climbing tower. Some of his friends destroyed his first attempt but, nothing daunted, he re-built it. He had a great struggle to fit one on top of the other. Having succeeded he then worked through the problem of climbing to the top of the three crates. He solved this by placing another crate next to them and by climbing up on to that one first. A short digression occurred here while he jumped off and re-mounted the first stage several times. After twenty-five minutes of wordless activity he collected together a number of miniature toy cars and the milk crates became a multi-storey car park; still no words, only occasional motor car noises.

Half way through this part of his play he was distracted by another child nearby who burst into tears. He observed this phenomenon dispassionately for half a minute. Then he returned to his fantasy game. One of the toy cars fell through the bottom of the upper crate so Mark dismantled the whole structure. He then attempted to make two towers and fix a bridge of crates between. He failed. Then he drifted away to join the tea party in the 'home corner', where he made pastry for ten minutes. He then decided to play in the sand. Observation ended at this point.

Mark was involved at many levels during this forty minutes. Building, matching, climbing, problem-solving, physical activity (jumping), fantasy (car park); and all these were his own ideas. No adult influence intruded upon him at any point. The episode is an indicator of the richness of the young child's powers of invention.

Keep an eye open when you are out and about. There are many equivalents of the milk crates which can be brought into the playgroup to add to the usual amenities; for instance, a couple of large cardboard cartons big enough for a child to get inside; or beer crates.

Children will play inventively with virtually everything that comes to hand.

Construction toys

By construction toys we mean manufactured toys especially designed as a set of parts which will fit together. Building kits are a good example. In choosing them remember that children's skill in using their hands will increase, so two basic kinds will be desirable. The simplest type of construction set has holes in various shaped blocks of wood, pegs to fix the blocks together, a wooden mallet and a pair of pliers. 'Matador' is an example of this type. Another is 'First Construction Set' obtainable in the U.K. from Galt's.

For the more advanced children there should also be a set which includes nuts and bolts to fix pieces together and a spanner (or wrench) to tighten them. 'Montage' is a good example.

Whichever toys of this nature are purchased it is as well to throw away the leaflet which suggests objects to be made with the apparatus. The children should feel free to use these toys in the same way as they would a collection of junk materials. That is, the primary experience should be the pleasure of fixing things together. No persuasion should be used to make a ship or a train or any specific object. If left to his own devices the child will eventually discover these things for himself. Amongst the things he will be likely to make will be the inevitable gun. He will probably want to rush round the hall shooting everybody. This will be disruptive to other play and may really frighten the timid children. The playleader should admire the gun, perhaps even allow herself to be shot, but should insist that the materials from which it was made be left in the construction corner, at the end of the game, for someone else to use. If this line is not taken it can happen that every child makes nothing but guns and this rather limits the use of the toy.

Other stimulating construction toys include 'Tinkertoy', and 'Playplax'. Playplax is specially valuable as it has the added attraction of transparent colour and it also poses problems of making the construction balance as it grows (fig. 27).

Fig. 27

Sound and music

The distinction between sound and music is a narrow one but it should be made in the playgroup. Both options should be provided either together or separately.

Listening skills

Many playleaders feel unsure of themselves in presenting musical experience to children. Sometimes they feel so unsure that they opt out of it altogether. This is a pity because there are many valuable but simple games which can be played with children which will increase their sensitivity to sound. Any adult, musical or not, can offer these.

In today's world of background noise, traffic, transistor radios, domestic and industrial machinery, children have plenty of practice in 'switching off' to sound. To restore the balance we need to give them opportunities to enjoy sounds and to differentiate between them. So let us look at some simple games.

Take two different objects, say a bunch of keys and a metal egg-cup. Begin by talking about them as everyday objects. Then rattle the keys and encourage the children to listen to the jingle. Then take any kind of implement which will serve as a musical beater and tap the egg-cup. Let the children listen to the ringing tone it makes. Extend the game by hiding the objects, perhaps in a cardboard box on your lap. With your hands inside the box and out of the children's sight 'play' one only and ask the children to decide which it is. The game might be developed over weeks by introducing other objects or by associating two objects slightly closer to each other in sound. Remember always to introduce the objects first so that the children can see them and become so familiar with their sounds that they are bound to be 'right' when asked to identify them. You will find many other everyday objects which make interesting sounds when suspended from a fine string and struck with a beater. Examples include a metal toast rack, a short piece of central heating pipe, a length of metal curtain-rail, or perhaps an old horseshoe if you live near a riding stable (fig. 28).

Shakers

Shakers can be provided in two ways. They can be made for the children, or they can be made by the children.

A two ounce instant-coffee tin is a conveniently sized container. When this is partly filled with rice, gravel or dried peas, painted a cheerful colour and the lid firmly stuck on with paint or a strong adhesive, an attractive piece of apparatus results. Such shakers can be made in 'sound pairs'. Every one in the set of six or eight looks exactly alike so that the children cannot pick out the pairs by sight but have to listen very carefully to the sound made by each in order to pair them.

Children are often overcome by curiosity and sooner or later if they are given ready-made shakers, as above, someone will want to know what is inside. He may even make great efforts to prize the lid off to find out. For this reason the playleader may prefer not to make the shakers for the children but to provide a selection of dried peas, rice, gravel, sugar, nuts and bolts, feathers and other suitable fillings and a number of transparent plastic pots with snap-on lids. Some dried herbs are sold in just such pots. She may then sit down at a table with a few children and talk about these materials. When the general talk has subsided she asks the children to find out what kind of noise is made when the fillings are put in the pots. Shakers are then made on the spot. Much conversation can follow about loud and soft noises or harsh and gentle noises. The children will offer suggestions as to what the sound reminds them of. Some will spontaneously dance around to the rhythm of their shakers.

Fig. 28

Imitating sound

Imitating sound also plays an important part in participating in music. The beginnings of this cannot be too simple from the children's point of view. Make any simple sound you like with your own voice such as 'bub, bub, bub, bub' or 'ooooooo' or 'ah ah ah ah'. Growl, groan or cry and anything other you can think of but make the vocal sound simple enough for the children to copy easily. They will love the game and will be learning a great deal about receiving, assimilating and imitating sounds. One or other of the children may offer sounds that he has made up. Accept them and you and the rest of the children do the repeating this time. This kind of imitation goes very well when linked to certain stories at story time. For instance, when the story is about animals imitate the sound the animal would make and let the children make it too. Make up a simple story including running, jumping, walking slowly. Clap out these rhythms each time they are mentioned. Some of the other children will quickly get the idea and will join in.

The movement session

Some dubious and virtually meaningless activities masquerade under the name of 'music and movement'. In attempting such activity we should take particular account of the age of the children. It is very easy to ask them to 'be' an animal or object which is quite outside their experience. The music provided may remind the adult of a queen, or a lion or an elephant, but what grounds do we have for supposing these under-fives will have similar thoughts? There may be a place for this kind of large group activity with the more mature four-year-olds, but we must guard against a too sophisticated approach.

At one highly successful session the children were shown a falling, twirling chiffon scarf. They began to interpret these movements with their own bodies and then the adult played music to fit their movements. This sort of combined activity is quite difficult for many playleaders. Do not worry if you never get so far as the large group movement session. Sing and try the simple listening games described earlier, plus others of your own invention. Once you get used to looking for them you will find all sorts of moments in the children's general play which are, really, experiments with rhythm. Good examples are a little girl who rhythmically banged her wrists together having first slid cylindrical Playplax pieces over her hands; the tap-tap of a hammer which was being beaten not for banging nails in but just as a source of rhythm; the thump, thump of four pairs of fists banging in unison and quite spontaneously at some dough. All these were sound, music and movement.

Fig. 29

Music

From the above it will be seen that we are already in the realm of music. Music should be thought of as an extension of sound activities. For a playgroup the following are the best musical accessories: drums, tambourines, coconut shells, bell sprays, triangles, castanets, chime bars (fig. 29), glockenspiel, xylophone, piano, cymbals, singing, claves (rhythm sticks), clappers, and wood blocks.

Do not attempt to provide too many musical accessories at once. Three or four are enough. All should be the genuine article, not toys. If tuned instruments are provided the tuning should be accurate. The young child's musical ear is vulnerable and may be corrupted by constant exposure to badly tuned instruments.

A piano for the children to strum on provides endless pleasure, but it too must be in tune. Chime bars are excellent in this respect. They never go out of tune. An octave of chime bars allows for experiment and exploration with musical intervals. If a triangle is too expensive hang a horseshoe and provide a six-inch nail as a striker. With a little ingenuity you can make other musical instruments.*

Do not be put off providing musical instruments because you consider music to be a difficult subject. If you place one or two within reach, ready to be explored, the children will try them out and in so doing will make sounds that they enjoy listening to. They will learn to differentiate between ordinary sound, noise, and musical sound. Take note of which they gravitate to, the music table or the sound table.

Left on his own a child may well pick out melodic patterns at the music table in exactly the same fantasy way as he will pick out patterns in paint if he is allowed to explore paint freely. Much can be learned about the child by watching the choices he makes; but only if they are his choices, unaffected by adult interference.

Listening to 'real' music

If there is a parent who plays a solo instrument the children will love him, or her, to come one day and talk about the instrument, and play it for a short time. This first-hand contact with instrumental music is very valuable and has much more meaning for small children than disembodied music coming from a record player. It is doubtful if very young children get anything from listening to records of orchestral music unless they have first had a great deal of experience in developing sensitivity to sounds. It is certainly not worth investing money in a record player for the playgroup. First-hand experience, as discussed above, however simple, has a great deal more meaning for most under-fives.

Records may well be useful for the adults to listen to in order to learn songs to pass on to the children. Some useful titles are:

50 All-Time Children's Favourites (traditional nursery rhymes), Wally Whyton, Hallmark Records HMA 218.

50 More All-Time Children's Favourites, Wally Whyton, Hallmark Records, HMA 229

Growing Up with Wally Whyton – 28 Kiddie Songs, Hallmark Records, HMA 245

---

* A useful publication here is *Making Musical Apparatus and Instruments* by K. M. Blocksidge, published by the Nursery Schools Association.

Songs from Play School, Decca, Ace of Clubs, ACL 1265
Songs to Grow on, Woody Guthrie, Transatlantic Records, XTRA 1067
Rhythms of Childhood, Folkways/Scholastic Records, 376–7653
Early Childhood Songs, Folkways/Scholastic Records, 376–7630
Folksongs for Young Folk, Folkways/Scholastic Records, Vol. I 376–7677, Vol. II 376–7642
40 of the World's Greatest Children's Songs, RCA, CAS–1017
The Wonderful World of Children's Songs, RCA, CAS–1079

Singing

Singing with young children is something we should all do whether we have a prima donna voice or not. Sometimes a nursery rhyme or song is sung to introduce a story or when children are gathered together for a sing-song time. There are also many moments during play which lend themselves to spontaneous singing. It need not always be a traditional rhyme. One child was showing her playleader how the water dripped slowly from the plastic bottle with the perforated base. Soon all the children were singing 'Raindrops are falling on my head' and thoroughly enjoying themselves all together. If we can introduce a degree of informality in our approach to singing we may prevent some children from growing up convinced that they cannot sing.

Literary activities

Story time

Provide a time when most of the children come together to listen to a story (fig. 30). This gives a good opportunity to build a feeling of comfort, of belonging to a group, and of a closeness between playleader and children. This does not mean that every child should be forced to sit with the group. Rather that there should be a time when the focus is on story-telling, in other words when it is obvious that a story is going on and most children will wish to join the group. Those who do not join in may play with any of the other quiet activities but should not be allowed to make so much noise that the story will be disrupted. The term 'telling' stories rather than 'reading' them is used deliberately. Where more than two or three children are listening it has been found that the presence of the book often distracts the children's attention. Some always want to bob up and down to see what is coming next. Also, when the reader's eyes are on the book and so averted from the children, atmosphere can be lost. If, however, the story-teller can find a version of a story she has learned by heart in a book with large clear illustrations it can add to the children's enjoyment if the book is held up facing them and they can look at the pictures as the story unfolds.

Another way to keep the children's full attention from the beginning is to have some 'props' available. For instance, you might sit in front of the young audience with something hidden in a large paper bag. As the bag is undone and a child's red sweater appears they begin to wonder what it is all about. General conversation may follow about jumpers and who is wearing a red one today. The story-teller then says, 'I know a story about this jumper.' The children will then be keen to hear 'The Little Red Jersey' from *Tell Me a Story*, a Puffin book of stories collected by Eileen Colwell.*

You will find many other easily available objects which may be used as the subject for a story in this way – but a word of warning on 'props'. If they are too exciting the children will want to handle them at once. This can be disruptive. It is best to establish the principle that 'props' are felt, and examined, *after* the story is finished.

It is not wise to tell the more horrific fairy tales to under-fives. In their world, reality and fantasy are so intermingled that they have difficulty in coping with witches and giants. In any case there is plenty of time for these stories later. They love stories with repetition, animal noises or actions, and

---

* Penguin, Harmondsworth, Middlesex and Baltimore, Maryland, 1962.

Fig. 30

stories concerning everyday occurrences with which they are familiar. A list of suggested sources of such stories can be found on page 110.

Perhaps the most important thing about choosing a story to tell is that the story-teller should enjoy the story herself. Apart from the obvious literary benefits from the group story children especially profit if they feel this to be *shared* enjoyment. From this point of view it is helpful if a second adult sits among the children showing wrapt attention and interest in what is going on.

The grouping of the children is essential to success at group story time. With anything from ten to twenty children it is helpful to have about half of them on chairs in a semi-circle and the others on a rug at their feet. In this way all the children remain in the story-teller's vision all the time and this increases the sense of involvement and of sharing the experience.

Book corner

If the playleader does not yet feel ready to try a group story, she need not deprive the children completely of the experience of listening to a story together. If she sits in the book corner and two or three children come to see what she is doing (fig. 31), the children will feel close and cosy while a story is read to them. This time they are all so close they are able to see the pictures in the book. The book does not come between reader and listeners in the way it would if used for the large group story.

Rota mothers are often happy to read to children in the book corner; but point out to them that a short chat, before they begin, about possibly unfamiliar things which may occur in the story, will greatly increase the child's understanding and so will be more likely to hold his interest. For instance, if you were to read *The Very Hungry Caterpillar* make sure they all know that caterpillars turn into butterflies. On the other hand, the events in stories like *Harry the Dirty Dog* are so completely within the child's experience that no prior explanations would be necessary.* A rapid glance at the pictures will quickly remind the adult which things may need talking about.

A list of some suitable books for the book corner will be found on page 109. It is important to display these books with their attractive covers showing and to make the whole corner as inviting as possible. This may be done by putting one or two small chairs there, with gaily covered cushions tied to the seats; or dispense with chairs and provide a bright rug plus, say, a cot mattress for which an attractive cover has been made.

It is most important that the children should always see clean and attractive books. This is where your public library will very likely help.

---

* Eric Carle, *The Very Hungry Caterpillar*, Hamish Hamilton, London, 1970; World Publishing Co., New York, 1970. G. Zion, *Harry the Dirty Dog*, Puffin Picture Books, Penguin, Harmondsworth, 1970; Harper & Row, New York, 1956.

Fig. 31

Public libraries

Many public libraries now lend up to twenty books at a time to groups for a half-term or longer. Sometimes librarians will come to playgroups to tell a story to the children, or to bring a film strip of a picture book. Such visits make exciting special occasions for the children but it is essential to discuss your requirements with the librarian before he or she arrives. It is sometimes necessary to point out that one film strip or story is enough for under-fives and that the position of the screen is most important. At one group the screen had been put so low that the children's heads threw exciting shadows on to the screen. The children discovered they could make shapes on the screen by bobbing up and down, and they loved it. Their self-discovered game would be an entertaining activity for another day, maybe, but it did not help concentration on the story.

Fig. 32

Nursery rhymes and finger plays

Van der Eyken in *The Pre-School Years* quotes infant school head teachers as saying that very few children come to school at five years old knowing the old traditional nursery rhymes. We should certainly include these in playgroup, sometimes said, sometimes sung; and perhaps buy *Mother Goose*, illustrated by Brian Wildsmith, and/or *Lavender's Blue*, edited by Kathleen Lines, for the book corner.*

To these traditional rhymes we should add 'finger plays'. These are rhymes led by adults and the children learn to accompany the words with actions using hands and fingers (fig. 32). If you are not familiar with finger plays get a copy of Elizabeth Matterson's *This Little Puffin*.** It contains a fine collection.

If the playgroup has a time when all the children come together for milk or orange this may be a good opportunity to introduce rhymes. But guard against an endless stream of rhymes going on and on just to fill in time. It is better if the theme from one rhyme suggests the next, if there is some continuity rather than an aimless hopping about from a rhyme about sausages, to one about squirrels, to another about soldiers! The disconnected approach will probably make less impact on the children than if one rhyme leads naturally to another.

Some time should be found each day for rhymes and stories or a vital opportunity to develop the children's natural love of words will be lost.

* *Mother Goose*, Oxford University Press, London, 1964; Watts, New York, 1965. *Lavender's Blue*, Oxford University Press, London, 1960; Watts, New York, 1954.

** *This Little Puffin*, Puffin Books, Penguin, Harmondsworth, Middlesex and Baltimore, Maryland, 1969.

Fig. 33

Games of fantasy

Home corner

The home corner (fig. 33) should be large enough for at least four or five children to play comfortably together inside it. It needs to be screened from the rest of the room so that the children feel that it is really their own house. On the other hand the screens should not be so high that they prevent the adult from making sure that no-one is being victimized, nor the playthings abused. Screens can easily be made by fixing hardboard to frames. They should be not more than 4 feet high (1·25 m) and may consist of two or three frames 4 feet by 6 feet (1·25 m × 1·80 m). They should be hinged for easy storage. It is essential that such frames are fixed to the wall to prevent them from falling over. Two stout hooks on the frame and two strong eyelets fixed into the wall are best. Some groups prefer not to make screens at all but to make use of the adult chairs which are such a constant feature in playgroup halls. About six of these should be placed side by side, with their seats facing inward, and about four placed in a row at right-angles to these. A curtain with a 'pocket' at the top is then made to cover two or three chairs at a time (fig. 34). The height of the curtain should equal the height of the chair backs. They should be made with deep pockets at the top to slip over the backs of the chairs. By accommodating two or three chairs at a time in this way the corner has a 'wall' around the outside and the seats of the chairs can become shelves, tables or what the children will. This type of home corner has been found to provide much more constructive play than the conventional type of small playhouse. The latter often only serves as a 'hidy hole' for the bully of the group to dare all comers, or for some timid small soul to hide away all alone. It does not offer enough space for groups of children and it is difficult for the adult to supervise it without intruding on the children's play.

Every home corner should have a child-size tea set, cookery set, small broom, dustpan and brush, and a toy iron and ironing board. A valuable additional item is a telephone. A real one can usually be obtained upon enquiry from your local telephone manager. His telephone number can be found in the front of your local directory.

If there is room in the corner for a 'bedroom' as well, so much the better. There are various ways of improvising beds large enough for a child to curl up on. Sometimes a large laundry basket is used. Sometimes two inverted plastic milk crates tied together with a piece of foam rubber on the top will serve. Sometimes a real cot is used, with one side permanently down. A dressing table may be made by putting a frill around the legs of a chair and tying a mirror to the back. Add to this a brush and comb and empty make-up pots and the girls – and some boys! – will thoroughly enjoy themselves.

Dolls and dolls' beds should also be provided and possibly prams. A small push-chair takes up less room than a pram and serves the purpose equally well. Dolls' clothes should be of simple design, preferably opening all the way down and fastened with velcro strips.

A nursing set bought from the toy shop may also be kept in the home corner. This will sometimes lead to 'hospital play'. It is best to buy a more expensive set as the cheaper variety last no time at all. If your group cannot afford a good set, put together some bandages, plasters, safety pins and empty ointment tins; put them in a neat box with a red cross on the outside.

Soft toys

These are not really suitable in the playgroup for three- to five-year-olds. Fluffy animals are such individual creatures that they do not lend themselves to group play. Young children usually have a favourite one at home and this they turn to frequently when in need of comfort, often when in need of mother. If mother is made part of the group by being welcomed as a helper at playgroup session, and if the initial separation from mother, when the child first comes to playgroup, has been well handled such comforters should not be necessary. The child will be far too busy climbing, painting, digging, building and experimenting with all manner of things.

Fig. 34

Play dens

Boys will often play in the home corner and will exchange roles quite happily with the girls. It is not unusual to see a robust lad dressed up in a frilly garment from the dressing-up box 'cooking' the lunch and being mother! However, if space allows, there should also be a play 'den' or 'cave', preferably well separated from the home corner, where the bigger boys can be encouraged to play if they get too boisterous for the home corner. Many halls used for playgroups have a large table which cannot be removed during play sessions. Do not think that it is taking up too much room. Cover it on three sides with a large cloth and it can become a 'den'. As a link with this area the playleader could place the large wooden crane, and the large 'Transporter Fleet' of large lorries and trucks, or the porter's trolley and pull-along-truck nearby. Next to that might be placed the woodwork bench.

In this way you can build up an area which will offer stimulating play of varying kinds to those vigorous boys who seem to want to do nothing but rush around the hall. Such planning, along with an area for physical apparatus, is particularly important when there is no outside play space.

Dressing up

All the children dress up. Why do they do it?

The words fantasy, imagination, and fantasy-play have appeared many times already in previous sections of this book but to none are they so appropriate as to 'dressing up'.

Very often the child will suddenly announce, 'I am a jet plane,' and to prove it he will swoop round and round with arms outstretched. Such is the power of imagination of the young child that, even without any 'props' except his arms, he imagines himself to be a jet plane. He jumps and is a frog. He moos and is a cow. He acts the part; he engages in primitive play-acting, drama, fantasy. His instinct for drama is the impetus behind such play.

The child's dramatic instinct can be enhanced by providing accessories. You will be surprised what comes to hand when you begin to look.

Hats

The fire brigade are very ready to donate old firemen's helmets. Try the police and the local Scout troop and see if they have any spare discarded head gear. Use that old pith helmet, that old soldier's tin hat, sailor's hat, airforce cap, top hat, bowler, boater. Ladies' fancy straw hats with flowers and artificial fruit on, particularly the wide-brimmed kind, are especially popular with the little girls. The attic may yield old trilbies and soldiers' ceremonial caps. Provide a large cardboard carton full of assorted hats and a large mirror firmly secured, at child height. Watch what happens. Policemen, firemen, soldiers, brides will all act out their roles. The little girl in fig. 35 has even managed to make a hat out of tinsel. In addition to the cardboard carton provide a sheet of pegboard with hooks to hang the hats on, so that the children can choose by looking.

Imitation plaits may be made by plaiting old stockings together and sewing one plait to each side of a hair band or ring of elastic. The child will enjoy changing her hairdo and her hat and so her personality.

Fig. 35

Clothes

Provide unwanted clothes, children's or adults', such as waistcoats, abandoned evening dresses and jackets, feather boas, shawls, sprays of artificial flowers or furs. Provide clothes which will fit all the children such as full skirts with elastic at the waist, capes fixed at the neck with small pieces of velcro, also stretch hairbands with bits of net and frills sewn to them for head-dresses. Belts of all colours and shapes will be popular and easily obtained from jumble sales.

The clothes should be hung on hangers, the wire type as from the drycleaners will do, and a rack at child height, about three feet high, could be made to hold them.

Do not allow the clothes to become too soiled.

Bit box

Fill a box with old lace and net curtains – white, black or coloured – pieces of floral material, lamé, feathers – the more colourful the better.

Try to amass a collection of other accessories such as sequined evening purses and handbags, coloured shopping bags, jazzy umbrellas and gloves. Shoes should be flat-heeled. Shoes with high or built-up heels are not very safe. The children may twist their ankles and the heels make a surprisingly loud noise in an echoing hall.

It is helpful to place the dressing-up corner next to the home corner; and do not forget the long mirror, set at the children's height, for them to admire themselves. An assortment of articles as outlined above is a constant and powerful source of inspiration to creative fantasies likely to lead a child to both self-expression and interaction with other children in group play.

Puppets

Young children enjoy glove puppets. The world of fantasy is so close to them that they become convinced that the creature held in the playgroup leader's lap really is a cat even though they can clearly see her arm disappearing into the glove. They will often hold a conversation with the puppet, or ask it questions, or invent things that have happened to it. The following took place in a playgroup in London. The playleader had a rabbit glove puppet on her lap. Jane crouched beside her.

Jane: 'Is your bunny sleepy?'
Playleader: 'Yes, she's a very tired rabbit.'
Jane: 'Has she been busy? I expect she has lots of baby rabbits to look after. My friend has a rabbit, she had ten babies. I wanted one. Mummy said we didn't have room.' (Smoothing the puppet.) 'She's not very soft. My friend's rabbit was soft. Poor bunny, are you cold? I'll get a blanket.' Jane fetches a blanket from the dolls' pram. 'There you are, that will keep you warm. Are you warm? She says she's warm, put her in the pram.'

Jane then took the 'rabbit' off the playleader's arm, wrapped her in the blanket, put her in the pram and pushed her around the hall for quite a long time.

The rabbit puppet quoted above was made from a cardboard Easter egg pushed into a white sock. Two pink ears were sewn on. Two red beads were used for eyes. The whiskers were made from bristles of a broom. A hole was made in the bottom of the egg to allow fingers to go into the head, and a dress was sewn firmly to the neck. It was simply made yet to Jane it was very real.

Jane was an articulate four-year-old. So perhaps this is the place to say puppets can be helpful in encouraging the less articulate child to talk. To achieve this the playleader would need to take a more active part than was the case with Jane, perhaps by saying 'She looks very tired. What do you think she's been doing?' thus sustaining the conversation herself. Or she could prolong the verbal encounter by pretending to be the rabbit speaking with the child. Some timid children seem to find it easier to speak to a puppet than directly to an adult, or even to another child. Such shyness is not uncommon when young children first enter a playgroup.

Some children will want to try their hand at working the puppets for themselves, but their hands get rather lost in an adult-sized glove. So make some special puppets, scaled down in size for small hands. Try putting them out in a box or on a ledge and see what happens.

Because puppets seem so real to under-fives, be careful which animals you choose to make. A very realistic crocodile was made like a sleeve to slip over the arm with a mouth which opened to show a red tongue and polystyrene teeth. It caused some real alarm among one group of children!!

The title of a recommended book on making puppets can be found in Further Reading on page 108.

Jig-saw puzzles

There is much to be said for the occasional use of games which keep children seated at table for a while. They reduce stress, abate noise and rest the child, and the adult!

Jig-saw puzzles are effective in this context. Children like them and will go to great pains to complete them. They should, however, feel they can ask the adult for help if they are unable to finish. The adult should then sit with the child and discuss which pieces might be needed next. It would be a mistake if the adult were to finish it off without involving the child. Working out the problem together brings a feeling of closeness between child and adult.

There are three main kinds of puzzle and children should have access to all as they represent progressive stages of difficulty.

The first type have whole shapes which lift out. Sometimes these shapes have knobs which enable the child to handle them more easily.

The second type show an object, for instance an animal, cut into individual pieces which can still be recognized as a complete head, or a leg, or a tail. It is important to provide this type because during assembly the shape of the individual piece is clearer for the young child than dismembered sections of the animal. Solving this type of simple puzzle constitutes a stage which many children need to experience before moving on to the third type.

The third type is the conventional puzzle in which a complete picture is cut into several pieces. This type is best if made in thick plywood and contained in a tray. If no tray is supplied one can easily be made by edging a piece of hardboard with quadrant beading.

Children should be encouraged to finish a puzzle if they start one. They should also be encouraged to clear it away when finished with, and clearing up is easier if the back of each jig-saw is painted in its own one individual colour. Each puzzle can then quickly be placed in its matching tray.

Jig-saws are valuable when children feel the need to destroy as well as to make, as they often do. The advantages of jig-saws is that the child can restore the status quo when he feels the need to. They also provide the child with an opportunity to test his ability to identify shapes and colours, particularly shapes.

Jig-saws may very well produce in a young mind a first grasp of concepts of space and number.

Other 'toy-shop' toys

If funds are short a playgroup does not need to spend money on commercially made toys at first, but there are some useful items which should be purchased once there is some money to spare. For instance boys will love a garage with toy cars. But, a word of warning about these; sooner or later one or other of the children will want to take them to the sand tray and to make roadways and tunnels and hills; and it will not be long before the damp sand will spoil the cars. To avoid this many playgroups buy two sets, one which the children know they are allowed to take into the sand and one which is kept for the garage. Alternatively, it is possible to buy plastic cars which are not spoiled by sand, and of these Tomte is a tried and tested brand.

In addition to cars a simple train set and layout of lines such as fig. 36, which is a Brio Miniature Railway, is also useful. Resist the temptation to stick the track to a piece of board in what *you* think is a beautiful layout. It may be easier to store but it will cut out much of the child's thought and imagination, by denying him the pleasure of fitting the rails together to his own pattern. One playleader who made such a layout wondered why the children stopped playing with the train. When finally she unstuck her carefully planned layout the children became interested again.

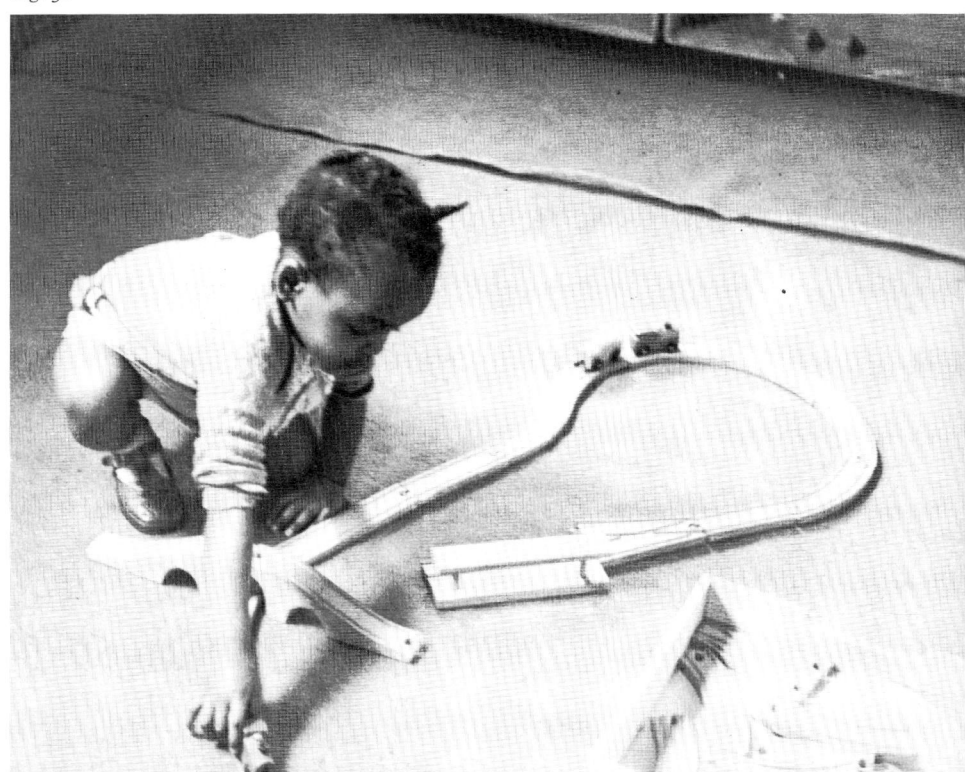

Fig. 36

A doll's house is a virtual necessity. When buying one choose the simplest style possible (fig. 37). As several children may wish to play at one time the 'open-sided' type or a number of separate rooms will be best. Choose solid simple furniture made from wood and provide a family of dolls – mother, father, boy, girl and baby. All of these are obtainable from Galt's and other good toy shops.

Fig. 37

Interest tables

When the playgroup is well established and the essential provisions of sand, water, paint, books, home-corner and physical apparatus are being used the playleaders should consider the possibility of finding a corner to set up an interest table. There may be a suitable shelf or ledge in the hall, or you may be able to free a table for the purpose. The main point to remember is that the objects should be displayed at a height where they can easily be seen by all the children.

There are two main kinds of interest table. One where the presence of an adult is essential; and the other where objects are put out for the children to browse among by themselves. In the second case the occasional presence of an adult is helpful in developing the children's thinking and conversation. If possible there should be a back-drop on the wall behind, and a cover over, the table before the objects are laid out so that the area is eye-catching and looks bright and attractive.

The objects set out should lead to conversation about their shape, texture, colour, and their use. If there is a theme running through objects set out at any one time the interest table will have more meaning for the children. Among the more unusual collections seen in playgroups recently are:

Brushes: hair-brush, clothes-brush, tooth-brush, shoe-brush.

Boots and shoes: father's shoes, baby's shoes, wellingtons.

Mirrors: on this were concave mirrors, convex mirrors, magnifying mirrors, two hand-bag mirrors fixed at right-angles to each other so that they reflected a small object an infinite number of times.

In addition to the mirrors, you could provide a simple home-made periscope, or a kaleidoscope (bought or home-made); a magical home-made piece of equipment for the mirror table can be made by acquiring a redundant painting roller. Strip off the lambswool or foam-rubber padding and replace it with small mosaic mirror-tiles. The children love pushing this backwards and forwards over coloured and patterned paper and watching the different reflections.

Another favourite object is the magnet. Make a collection of as many different kinds of magnets as can be found, bar, horseshoe, and round magnets; magnets out of old loud-speakers. Try to get them of varying magnetic strengths. Keep a box of metal bits and pieces for the magnets to pick up. Also include on the magnet-table magnetic toys such as 'battling rams', 'moving ladybirds' and games like magnetic fishing. The children will be fascinated by the apparently magical powers of the magnets and will, incidentally, be learning something about magnetism.

Battery boards

Battery boards provide the child with a great deal of interest. Take a block of wood about ten inches square. Fit a suitable battery in one corner and a torch bulb in a holder in another corner. Fix a wire from one side of the battery to the bulb. Put another from the other side of the bulb to the other side of the battery but do not fix it (fig. 38a). The children will soon discover that the bulb lights when the bare end of the wire touches the other terminal tag on the battery.

A second board could be made in the same way but this time with both wires fixed to the battery and one wire interrupted by a small switch (fig. 38b).

On a third board there could be a gap in the wire instead of the switch (fig. 38c). A box of bits and pieces of metal, plastic, wood, cork, should be available some of which, as the children will find out, will carry the current across the gap, and some will not. Let the children discover which is which and so learn the facts about, if not the words, conductor and insulators.

Make a fourth board like the first but substitute a buzzer for the bulb. Do not be afraid of the words 'electricity' and 'battery'. They are perfectly safe for children to use.

Almost every object in existence is of interest to young children. You will think of many other collections for your interest tables which will focus attention on a related family of objects for a few days and so begin the process of sharpening the children's perception of the world around them.

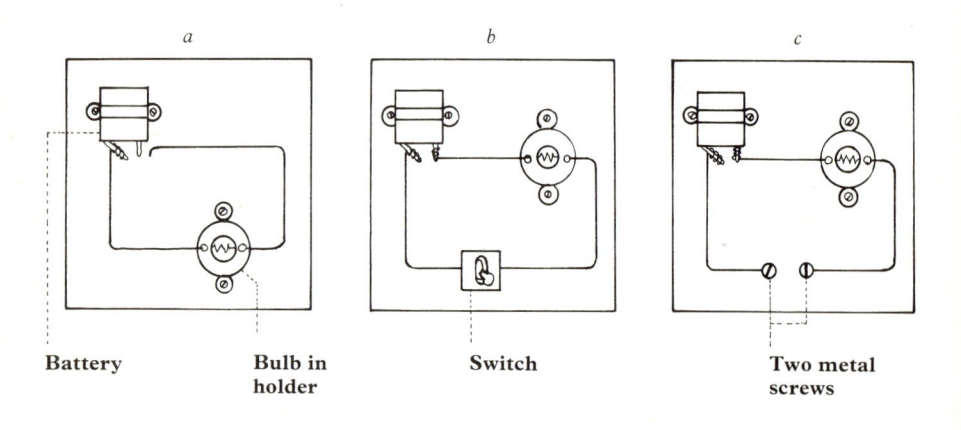

a   *b*   *c*

Battery   Bulb in holder   Switch   Two metal screws

Fig. 38

Radio and TV table

The remains of an old TV or radio set will provide much interest for the children. If such are provided the 'tube' and all glass valves must be removed. But when you remove the tube from a television set, do be careful how you dispose of it. If fractured it will explode, or, more accurately, it will implode and glass fragments will fly about dangerously. Television repair shops sometimes have old sets or parts of sets which they are willing to give away and the kind-hearted ones will usually remove the tube for you (fig. 39).

After they have been made safe the sets may be put on a low table with a varied assortment of screwdrivers and any other available suitable small tools. Fantasy soon takes over. The children will be convinced they are

Fig. 39

mending the set. They will even tell you the programme they can see. A child, quite unaware of the adult's presence, talked to himself in the following way while turning the screws. 'This plug won't work. I must mend it. Push that knob up there. If I take that wire, that will make it better. There! Now it works!' He continued to play at this table for a further thirty minutes (fig. 40).

A good addition to the radio and TV table is a box of old electrical and mechanical bits and pieces, old plugs, bells, wires, junction boxes, even bicycle bells, bits of clocks and watches and so on. Some people worry that this provision will encourage the children to break or unscrew objects in general use in the home. There is no evidence of this. On the contrary, if the children have their own property to experiment with they are less likely to tamper with things in the home.

Fig. 40

Attended interest tables

As mentioned earlier some interest tables require the constant presence of an adult if their purpose is to be achieved. Here are some examples.

Dissolving table

Sit beside a table on which you have placed two jugs of water, some plastic tea-spoons, some empty jam jars and some small plastic pots containing substances which dissolve at different rates, e.g. soda, icing sugar, granulated sugar, salt, bicarbonate of soda and perhaps something that will not dissolve at all, such as gravel. It will not be long before several children come to look. When they do you can talk to them about the various substances. Ask if they would like to find out what happens when water is added. The children then choose a substance, put a little from the plastic pot into the jam jar, add water and stir. Keep a good store of bicarbonate of soda handy because this one is always very popular once its fizzing properties have been discovered!

Mixing table

Put out about four tall clear glass bottles and fill them with water. Have on hand a number of small bottles or jars containing red and black ink, milk and liquid food colouring. You will also need some medical 'droppers' – most mothers will have at least one of these handy! Let the children take a dropper and draw up some liquid of their choice. This they then let fall, a little at a time, into one of the full large bottles. It will not mix at first but will twist and curl and make patterns as it finds its way through the water. This is magical to the children and they will watch fascinated.

When the activity is over the children should empty their bottles into a bucket put there for the purpose beside the table. Large jugs of water should be kept ready for the next children to fill their bottles.

Some grocers sell icing colouring in plastic dropper bottles. You may find it easier for the children to use these rather than the medical droppers.

'Smelling' table

Arrange small jars on a table containing substances with very different smells, e.g. vinegar, coffee, a small piece of onion, perfume, hand cream. Sit by the table and children will soon gather round. Their reactions to the various scents will be sharp and remarkable!

Colour corner

The child is never too young to be exposed to influences which help him to develop. He grows physically, mentally and emotionally all the time. He also matures in other, subtler ways. For instance, his senses become more acute and he grows more receptive to external stimuli provided by touch, smell, taste, sound and, above all, sight.

Confront a child with an easel and paint and painting materials and one of the effects upon him, when he uses the paints, is that he will begin to develop visual awareness of, and interest in, colour. Later in life he will need a developed sense of colour, so it seems prudent to begin early to lay the foundations. In other words early experience of colour is beneficial. Painting provides direct practical involvement with colour.

The colour corner is another, subtle, way of providing a different kind of colour experience for the child.

A colour corner is, as the term implies, a corner for coloured things. It is usually set up as a display of coloured objects. In practice it is generally made up of all the same colour, e.g. yellows: pale, dull, bright, acid, cool, hot and so on. The background should be made up of yellows, and the ground likewise. The objects could be a lemon, a yellow flower, a yellow pencil, a yellow plate, a yellow book, a yellow ball, a yellow hat. The background could be strips of figured wall paper; the ground a yellow check table cloth, a patch of shiny yellow paper or whatever else is available (fig. 41). Such a collection makes an impact on the environment and upon the child, especially if he is allowed to handle the objects.

There is an unknown factor in all this. It is the degree to which the child will experience the colours, if at all. Colour differentiation will be possible for some young children and not for others. Yet, even though the effects cannot be accurately assessed it is still worth setting up a colour corner. Even very young children will stand and look and touch, the shiny, the round, the smooth, the bobbly, and they will dream. That is enough, at their age.

Fig. 41

Fig. 42

Nature

If it is possible set up a nature table each week, but if space does not permit let it take weekly turns with an interest table or colour corner (fig. 42).

Plants

It is best to limit activities to plants which will grow naturally and well in the conditions you have on your own particular premises.

Bulb planting in fibre, or cultivating, by resting them on the neck of a jar of water is a suitable procedure for the playgroup. It helps to keep the bulb water fresh if a little charcoal is added to it. For quick results, which the children delight in, it is difficult to beat mustard and cress grown according to the instructions on the packet. In due time this activity provides the children with filling for sandwiches. The achievement of a 'crop' carries their interest far beyond merely growing things.

Another quick-result activity is to line a jam jar with blotting paper, put a little water in the bottom of the jar and then fix a broad bean seed between the side of the jar and the blotting paper. Root and shoot will soon appear if the blotting paper is kept damp. From then on growth is rapid.

Twigs can be brought into the playgroup at the different seasons of the year. But it is better still if the children can be taken on an outing to collect specimens. They love the story of how the horse-chestnut tree got its name. They are fascinated by the sticky feel of the buds and by discovering the minute rolled-up leaves as the outer casing is taken off. The adult can point out the scar where last year's leaf fell off just below the bud, and its resemblance to a horseshoe. Try to keep a real horseshoe available for comparison.

In one playgroup the children had spent part of the morning planting crocus bulbs. At the end of the session one child sat gazing at his pot. He remained like this for such an unusually long time the playleader felt impelled to intervene. 'Tell me what you are doing Tom,' she said. 'I'm waiting for it to grow,' he answered pointing to his crocus. He was obviously under some misconception. Perhaps an unwary helper had said, 'If we plant some bulbs they will grow.' So Tom, lacking experience, expected instant action. The boundaries of the child's knowledge at the age of three are limited. 'If we plant them they will grow, but it will take a long time, two or three weeks,' would have been more helpful to Tom.

But perhaps he was not put on the wrong track by an adult. Perhaps it was just simple lack of knowledge and he was revealing his faulty grasp of timing.

The young child's sense of time is one of the last to develop.

There are many such apparently simple play incidents, and the child's remarks about them, which reveal significant information about his mental development. We cannot afford to miss any of them.

Tadpoles and others

Some small living creatures may be kept in playgroups providing they can be given conditions in which they can survive. It may be possible to get frog-spawn in early spring and to hatch it into tadpoles; but remember tadpoles prefer rainwater to tapwater and also bear in mind that tadpoles need to eat. If you cannot get pond weed feed them with an occasional lettuce leaf, or a small piece of raw meat. Make it quite clear to the children that once the tadpoles turn to frogs it would be cruel to try to keep them indoors. Arrange an outing for one or two of the older ones to go with you to free the frogs in the nearest pond.

Earthworms can also be kept indoors. Take a rectangular fish-tank or something similar and get the children to fill it with alternate layers of sand and brown earth. Put a layer of damp leaves over the top and you will have a good home for several earthworms. If you cover the sides with black paper the worms will work near the glass walls. When the paper is removed after a few days the children will be able to see the tunnels the worms have made and how they have mixed the sand and earth.

Snails and insects

If you have any outdoor space, however small, let the children use it as a hunting ground for living things, particularly in spring and summer. The most unpromising area will often yield snails, woodlice, ants, ladybirds. The children's excitement in discovering them has to be seen to be believed. Even tarmac areas sometimes allow a plant to push through, and insects are often to be found there, or in the cracks and crevices of brick walls.

Domestic pets

If possible keep a hamster or guinea-pig, or rabbit, as the group pet. The children will gain all the advantages of caring for and looking after a creature which is smaller than themselves and in need of their care and protection. Most pet shops stock booklets on the care of pets. Buy the appropriate one and study it before you purchase any pet.

For the many groups that do not have facilities for keeping pets it may be possible for an animal and his owner to visit the group for part of a morning. The most enterprising venture seen recently was when Jackie's mother took ten baby rabbits to the playgroup. The children had a lovely time feeding them, stroking them, even taking them for rides in the push chair. They were all returned safely to Jackie's older brother, to whom they belonged.

It would, perhaps, not be advisable to have a large bouncy dog for a playgroup visit. The timid children might find him a bit much! However, it is particularly helpful to have children who have no pets of their own to come into contact with live animals.

One final thought, at the end of this section on living things. Nature deals with nothing if not with 'life'. It is better to have no nature table than to have a dead one.

Fiddle-board

As soon as the child can propel himself around by instinct he 'gets into everything'. He turns every knob, presses every button, switches every switch, rattles every chain, opens doors, pulls everything, pokes his finger into every hole, sometimes with lethal results if the electric sockets are not child-proof. A child is an adventurous creature, full of curiosity, an explorer of all the minute details in his immediate vicinity. Every prudent mother, or other responsible adult, will keep a wary eye on his interest in dangerous items such as power-plugs, gas taps, open fires. If she is wise she will encourage his other, safer explorations as a means of his coming to terms with his environment. She may even make positive use of the child's natural inclination to fiddle about with things by persuading her handy husband – handy husbands are a most valuable asset to any playgroup – to make a fiddle board (fig. 43).

It is a board say 24 inches by 18 inches (60 cm × 45 cm) to which are fixed as many movable, soundable, twizzleable bits and pieces as the garage, the tool shelf and the junk-box will provide. In the illustration Alex, aged 2 years 10 months, is busy at a board which has, fixed to its surface, wheels, cogs, a door bolt, a door knocker, a spiral spring, a battery-operated buzzer, a cycle bell, a cycle hooter, a zip-fastener, hinges, terminals, an old grandfather clock's chiming coil, a chair caster, a small light bulb and battery, a bell-push. Assembled as they are on the board in this way he can fiddle with all of them as long as he likes in perfect safety.

The fiddle-board is a piece of equipment which takes, and channels, and enlarges upon one part of the normal child's instinctual behaviour pattern, his yen to explore and be curious; it begins with the child.

The first time we saw a 'fiddle board' was in Winchester in September 1971. It was made by a playgroup father and was included in an exhibition of commercial and home-produced playgroup equipment which was part of a Playgroup Conference in that city. We acknowledge the fiddle board idea to that source.

Fig. 43

Outings

Simple outings, with just a few children, can be of immense value if they are led by a sensitive adult who will talk with them about the experience, and follow it up through books, activities, and conversation in playgroup later on. Either the supervisor or her assistant should take about six children out at a time. A mother can then be invited to take the absent helper's place in the hall for that morning. It should be borne in mind that parents' permission must always be obtained before the children are taken out of the group. Also make sure your insurance policy covers children while they are on outings.

The following examples give some idea of the variety of purposeful outings which can be contrived. All have been noted from actual experience in various playgroups; before cookery six children were taken to the grocer's to buy the ingredients. On such a trip there would be opportunity to talk about pedestrian crossings, traffic, money, and the foodstuffs in the shop.

The books needed renewing in the book corner. A few children were taken to the public library to help choose more.

The book corner needed brightening up, so a trip to the nearest florist was arranged.

This spontaneous kind of outing can be undertaken with very little preparation, and usually, even for the more elaborate visits, such as to the local fire station, all that is needed is a phone call a few days in advance. The children are invariably made welcome by the firemen and are often allowed to sit in the engine, and perhaps try on the helmets. One group arranged for a fire engine to come and park beside the playgroup hall and children were taken out in twos and threes to look over it. The same group followed this up with a similar visit from a police car. Now the local constable frequently drops in for a 'pretend' cup of tea in the home corner. Members of the police force are often keen to make contact with young children in this way, perhaps as a means of fostering good relations between police and public.

If the police visit the playgroup it is probably better for the children to show them round. Children of this age will not absorb very much from just sitting in a group listening to talks about road safety.

Many groups make use of local parks for outings. It is sometimes helpful to set a simple task as a purpose for the visit, for example to collect fallen leaves. On return to the hall let those who want to – but do not force anybody – sort the leaves into types, or sizes, put them on the nature table, or use them for collage.

When thinking in advance about arranging outings for your children scour your own neighbourhood for possibilities. One group in the heart of London is near, believe it or not, a windmill. This is unexpected and exceptional. It would be hardly surprising if there is nothing of this nature in your area, but there might easily be a bus depot, or a railway station or a garage where cars are repaired.

Remember to make use of events which occur unexpectedly, like the men who arrive to dig up the pavement outside the hall, or to clean the street lights, or demolish the building two streets away. Children are endlessly fascinated by other people's work and the machinery used to pursue it.

Often such outings will suggest a subject for that day's story time. For instance a visit to a building site could well be followed by the story in *Little Pete Stories* by Leila Berg.*

Outings will always mean more to children if you take out just a few at a time and if you too look interested and excited.

---

* *Little Pete Stories*, Young Puffin, Penguin, Harmondsworth, 1970; Verry, Lawrence, New York, 1964.

Physical activities

Young children are so full of physical energy that unless they are given an outlet for it there is almost bound to be trouble. The child who has nowhere to run and climb, and generally let off steam, will often use his surplus energy in dashing round and spoiling the games of others. Ideally, each playgroup would have its own outdoor space but, unfortunately, this is not always the case. It is therefore important when arranging the various areas in the playroom, to leave an area clear and free for the children to jump, balance, and climb. It is also necessary to have a good variety of apparatus to encourage them to develop and extend bodily skills.

The Variplay Triangle Set (fig. 44), is a good investment in this respect because it can be put to a variety of uses. A child has to get the help of a friend to arrange the planks, or to push him on the wheeled sections, or to work the see-saw, and this encourages interaction and cooperation.

Fig. 44

Tyre trolleys are popular too. These can be bought, but may also be made by a handy father. A piece of stout $\frac{3}{4}$ inch plywood (1·8 cm) is fixed to one side of an old car tyre and four casters are screwed to the outside face of the plywood. The children can then sit inside and push each other about the room, or can fill the trolley with bricks or any other handy cargo for transportation from one end of the room to the other.

Many children enjoy the climbing frame. There is a popular model which is made of wood and folds up. It is particularly suited to playgroups where apparatus has to be cleared away each day, and where weight is an important consideration.

As distinct from a climbing frame use a wooden ladder-bridge, such as can be obtained in the U.K. from Galt's, or a metal version from R. Whittle Ltd. This gives more opportunity for children to test the strength of their arms by swinging from the bars. As a piece of apparatus it also offers greater variety. A slide is a valuable addition to any climbing frame and should be provided where space allows.

If there is a safe and handy beam or bar in the hall throw a rope over and suspend a sack full of waste paper, tied securely at the neck, and let the big, over-active boys pummel away at it. They will burn up excess energy and get much healthy physical satisfaction out of it.

Some groups have small trampolines for the children to bounce on. Some caution is necessary if one is provided. There have been instances where such apparatus has caused accidents. The handle is a hazard, particularly to teeth though this can be lessened to some extent by padding it with foam rubber.

Manufacturers are now producing strong plastic open-ended barrels which produce all kinds of exciting play, amongst which is 'crawling into' and 'crawling through' – in other words tunnelling. The barrels are preferable in some ways to the long, cloth-covered hide-away tunnels which can lead to difficulties. Sometimes a burrowing infant is held captive in one of these while his two 'friends' twist each end tightly, thus preventing him from getting out, a distressing experience for the prisoner.

Pedal cars and tricycles can also lead to difficulties where there is no outside playspace. In a hall there is rarely room to use them as they are meant to be used. On the whole they seem to get in the way of the climbing frame and other more constructive playthings.

If the cost of climbing frames and Variplay Triangle Sets is too high children need not be deprived entirely of agility apparatus. A supply of stout cardboard boxes does very well to climb over and into. They are not very durable so should frequently be replaced. An ordinary plank set up on two house bricks will do very well for practising balancing skills.

Try to reserve one corner for a large gym mat. The modern type made of one-inch thick Recticel, or thick plastic foam, is good. This invites all kinds of tumbling, rolling and jumping movements which may not otherwise take place, or, if they do, may happen among other activities and so disrupt the play of other children.

Large balls, hoops and bean-bags are useful out of doors or, right at the end of the morning, indoors if you really have to clear most of the activities away before the children have gone home. It is best to put out a choice of all the activities until after the children have left, but not infrequently the hall has immediately to change function, perhaps to be ready for meals for the elderly or some such purpose. In this case rather than have the hall completely empty of toys for the last ten minutes of the session offer the children balls, hoops, bean-bags, and quoits. They will find any number of ways of using them and they can be gathered up quickly and put away as the children are taken home.

Language

All the activities described in this book help the child to understand the world around him. Through experiment and experience they give him a chance to play out his fantasies and the means to develop his rapidly increasing bodily skills. In a good playgroup he will also develop an understanding of the needs of others, and a certain amount of independence.

In addition there will be opportunities for speech and language development. Much of this will occur naturally in his play with other children, especially as some of his friends will be more advanced in language than he is.

The sensitive playleader, or parent, will find many other opportunities for encouraging the children to use language. The presence of an interested adult is often, in itself, enough to stimulate the child to talk about the things he is playing with, or to describe what he has been doing outside the group.

Children seem to find dough a relaxing play material. If the playleader or a mother takes a small chair and sits at the dough table the children will often begin to chat. The adult can, and should, stimulate the development of such conversations where appropriate; but guard against asking direct questions to which there is a 'right' or a 'wrong' answer. Far from encouraging the child to speak this may make him so unsure of himself that he will not risk speaking at all for fear of being wrong.

As has been mentioned elsewhere, stories, puppets, books, interest-tables and many other activities play a positive part in increasing vocabulary and encouraging children to talk.

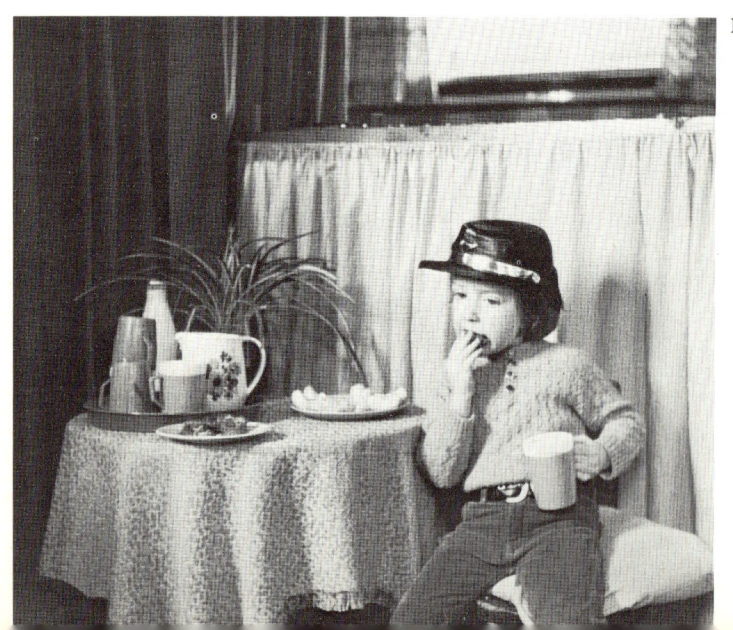

Fig. 45

Fig. 46

Milk time talk

Another good moment for conversations is at milk or orange juice time (fig. 46). Playgroups deal with refreshments, generally speaking, in one of two ways. Sometimes all the children come together about mid-morning and a drink plus a suitable snack is provided. This is a good social time and a natural setting for conversation, always bearing in mind that we must try to find ways to induce all the children to take part. We should not expect the majority to sit, each day, listening to the same one or two children giving their news. We must also be careful not to let this time go on too long. Some groups set aside a milk corner with a table and perhaps four chairs. Milk is put out about 45 minutes after the children arrive and it remains out for about an hour. During that hour children come, in twos and threes and *sit down* to drink (fig. 45). They are likely then to chat to their companions or to a mother, or playleader when she can find time to sit there too. This second alternative is more intimate than the large milk circle.

If the corner can be made to look special, perhaps with a bright table cloth or a colourful picture on the wall, it may be, even more, a stimulus to conversation.

It is right that we should make special use of the opportunities for speech which playgroup provides but playleaders must be careful to pick the right moment. If the child is deeply involved in what he is doing, perhaps with the clay, pinching, poking, thumping it, it would be inappropriate for an adult to swoop down and engage him in conversation. To do so would be to destroy the engrossing experience provided by the clay at that moment. If he were so suddenly disturbed he would probably dash off to some other activity, his concentration having been broken.

Moreover, a child must be well settled emotionally before extended efforts are made to encourage language development. Some children, even after they have given mother permission to go, are still very anxious for a while. They may need to talk to the playleader at this time. More usually they seem to like to remain quietly taking things in. It is better at this stage to let them feel really at home by getting 'lost' in the water, paint, sand or whatever else they choose, rather than to overpower them with too much talk.

With experience each playleader will be able to judge when a child is ready to be encouraged a step further forward. In groups where the playleaders have learnt to encourage, without interfering, children mature in all sorts of ways which are not apparent in groups where the declared aim is simply to allow the children to let off steam. These latter groups produce far fewer children who reach the maturer stages of drawing and painting, fewer who can concentrate even for short periods, and fewer who can talk about their play.

It may be thought that this does not matter but if playgroups are to be more than child-minding centres the question playleaders should be continuously asking themselves is 'When do I stand well back, and when does he need my support?'

Practicalities

The value cannot be urged too strongly of occasional meetings where parents and supervisors can discuss freely the aims and objectives of the playgroup. It is particularly important to have one such meeting for parents of new children before the child joins the playgroup. Many aspects of the work can then be explained. Not least important one can enter a plea to parents to bring their children suitably clad, and not in their 'party best' as sometimes happens.

Nevertheless, however washable the children's clothes may be, it is reasonable to expect the playleader to take sensible precautions against mess of all kinds and damage to clothes in particular. For all activities in which clothes could suffer the children should wear plastic aprons which, eventually, they can learn to put on and take off for themselves. A working party of mums could make these quite simply from PVC or old plastic rain macs (fig. 47). The shape illustrated in the drawing has proved to be convenient. The edges should be bound and the ends of the waist band should be provided with a fastening of velcro. The child can put his head through the hole with the shorter part hanging down his back. He then brings the waistband ends together round the front and fastens them by pressing them together. If the aprons which are used for water play have a band of foam plastic stuck across the lower edge it prevents water running straight into shoes. Some groups prefer to have sleeves as well, with elastic at the wrists,

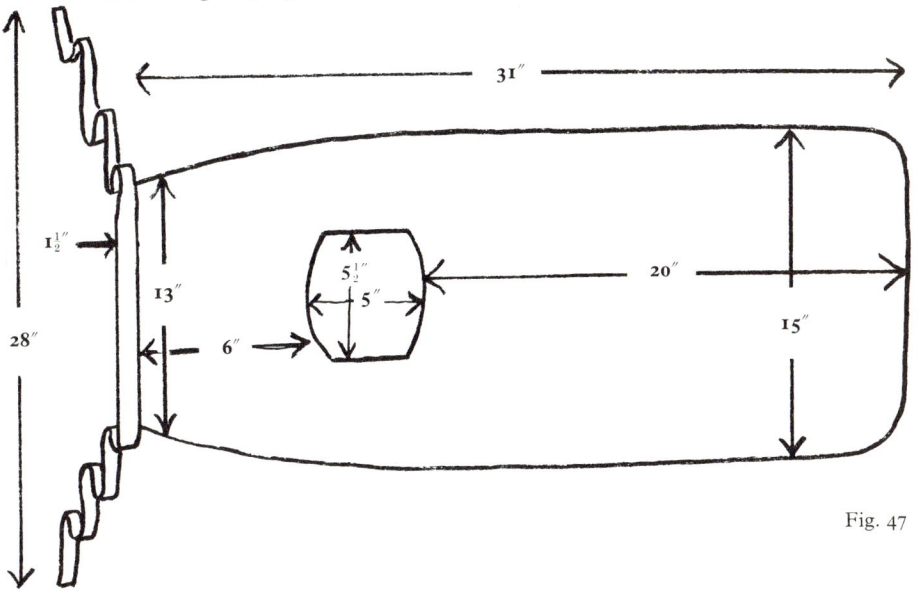

Fig. 47

for water play. These inhibit the children's freedom of movement somewhat. It is probably enough to push sleeves well above the elbow.

Aprons should always be hung near the activity for which they are intended, at a height the child can easily reach. On painting easels it is a good idea to fix a cup-hook at either end, at the top, each to take one apron.

Just as the children's clothes need care and protection so too does the floor of the hall. A groundsheet is an efficient covering. Heavy-duty polythene is also suitable. To prevent the polythene from getting pulled about and creased, tack a thin strip of wood down the long edge. When play is over roll the plastic on the strip for easy storage.

Children should always be encouraged to help in the clearing-up (fig. 48). For activities like finger painting it is vital to have a bucket, and large sponges for wiping tables. Put them in the corner where the children are working. This corner should also have a bowl and paper towels, on the spot, for hand washing. It is very tempting for a four-year-old, if he has to walk the length of the hall to wash his sticky or paint covered hands, to try a few hand prints on the way, on a wall, or even on furniture which may be used later by members of other organizations who share the use of the hall.

It is important that the tables provided should be not more than 20 inches (50 cm) high, and that chairs are in proportion to this. Many playleaders have to make do with adult furniture for the children's use. If this is the case they should try the experiment of going round the hall making a careful survey of all apparatus at eye level of the smallest child in the group. Try this, and judge whether the room looks exciting and inviting from the child's viewpoint.

Mops and absorbent cloths should be available near water play for the children's use and a large dustpan and soft brush near the sand.

Attention to such domestic details helps the children to achieve a sense of responsibility and also helps to maintain good relations with caretakers and owners of premises. It may even help to keep the rent down!

Premises

It is often the case that there is only one hall in the district and this has to serve all sorts of purposes for miles around. If, however, there is a choice of accommodation try to find premises for the playgroup with outdoor space (fig. 49). Young children need fresh air. It is possible to allow more boisterous play out of doors. Riotous play within the confines of the hall will make too much noise and will upset some children.

Fig. 48
Fig. 49

Extra room

Try to find a hall with an extra room for occasional use. Such a room gives a group much more flexibility. It could be used as a retreat for a small group of children, or as a meeting place for mothers. Mothers may wish to meet for a cup of coffee or tea while their children are playing and cases of adult loneliness and shyness can be overcome in such a group. If there is an extra room in the playgroup hall it would be possible to take advantage of facilities provided by some adult education institute and evening classes where a tutor can be sent to the playgroup to talk with mothers on any subject from child development to flower-arranging. Without doubt an extra room is a desirable asset in extending the work of a playgroup.

Storage

Storage is always a problem in shared premises. Check carefully how much storage space you will be allowed before you agree to use the hall.

A useful piece of storage furniture to buy is a hinged, lockable, unit about 2 feet 6 inches high, 3 feet long and 12 inches deep (75 cm × 90 cm × 30 cm). If your group cannot afford to buy such a unit, it is well worth trying to find a father who can make one (fig. 50). It is ideal for storing jig-saws and other table toys. The children choose what toys they want from it and should be encouraged to put them back when play is over. It helps if each drawer is labelled with a picture of the toy which is kept in it. This type of storage unit has more than one use. Opened right out the back of it can make one wall of a home-corner. Set at right-angles it can make a quiet corner for playing with the toys it contains. It can be useful in display.*

The keynote of successfully equipping and running a playgroup consists in taking a practical view of problems. This means being prepared to try out established procedures and to experiment with new ones. It means enlisting the help of all interested and willing adults. Much goodwill is shown by the general public towards the playgroup movement. Much support is usually forthcoming, often from unexpected sources.

Look in a practical way at the needs and ask for help.

---

* Plans and instructions for a home-made version may be found in the pamphlet *Making Playgroup Equipment*, available from Pre-School Playgroup Association, Alford House, Aveline Street, London SE11 5DJ.

Fig. 50

Present and future

This book has dealt with two aspects of play, first 'play as play', and secondly 'play in the playgroup and its social significance'. The approach is practical though it is hoped some philosophical inferences will be drawn.

All the activities which have been outlined, whether practised by the child in the playgroup or at home, are play activities or play-inducing activities and they should be seen as falling into a number of distinct, but linked, categories, as follows:

Art and craft activities: these induce creative and expressive play with paint, drawing, paper, sticky, clay, junk and other materials, sand, bricks, sound, musical instruments.

Literary activities: these enable the child to play with words, using voice sounds. They demonstrate word patterns in nursery rhymes and word play, and in the subtle mental rhythms of stories whose structure depends upon cumulative repetition; 'This is the house that Jack built', etc.

Fantasy: the play of imagination, and magic, fill more than half the child's world in the first few years. Dressing-up especially falls under this heading.

Visual stimulation: the presentation of visual materials, mechanical and natural, promotes discovery play. Good examples are colour corners and interest tables.

Physical activity: this is the play category most easily recognized and appreciated by the adult whether encountered at home or in the playgroup. The good playgroup caters effectively for the physical needs of the young child.

Play is part of the pattern of developmental behaviour. The greater the diversity, and the richer the quality, of play the surer will be the growth of the child towards intellectual, emotional, social and physical maturity. Playleaders would do well to avoid 'teaching' in the playgroups and to concentrate on the 'educational spin-offs' of playgroup play.

The two main requirements for under-fives are a stimulating diet of play and a secure emotional environment in which to take full advantage of that provision. These requirements may be met in a variety of ways. The differing needs of families with children under the age of five could not possibly be met by one uniform provision. It is to be hoped therefore that there will always be different kinds of schemes so that parents may take advantage of that situation which best suits them and their children. The government White Paper H.M.S.O. 5174, December 1972, 'Education, a Framework for Expansion', recognizes by implication the positive contribution that British playgroups have made in promoting social awareness of the value of the young child's play. In addition it expresses the hope that 'playgroups will continue to have a distinctive and valuable role to play alongside an expanding system of nursery education'.

There is a widespread and growing interest, in the United States, in the total welfare of very young children. The Day Care and Child Development Council of America Inc., for instance, has the same ultimate aims as the British playgroups movement has for the welfare of the very young child, and the involvement of parents. It is probably true to say that circumstances vary from state to state in America; but one hard fact emerges. Senior American Social Workers and Educators are increasingly visiting British Playgroups, and considering their social implications, in their study tours of Britain. The authors have already been involved in compiling itineraries to facilitate such studies.

We hope that British local authorities will support the white paper and will find ways to ensure that playgroups *do* continue. The best of them offer a unique opportunity for parents to exercise direct responsibility in the planning of provision for their under-five children. Many parents, especially mothers, have found personal satisfaction, and hidden resources within themselves, as a result of attending playgroup courses, by learning how to organize their own committees, choose equipment, and work alongside the playleader. A most significant aspect of the work of playgroups is the degree to which parents can, if they wish, become involved. It would be regrettable if this opportunity, already yielding such rich results in terms of parental understanding and community relations, were to be discontinued.

Still in the context of parental involvement; in another form it has a subtler function. The child's play will be of greater value if he feels that his parents share it with him. It is therefore important for parents to take every opportunity to help at play sessions, and to share in the running and organization of the playgroups. By doing so they can see what is provided for play. They can carry ideas away and adapt them for use in their own homes. Most children are in playgroup for only two and a half hours a day for thirty-nine weeks of the year. This is a small part of their total lives. The good work achieved in the playgroup will be consolidated if there is some 'carry-over' of their experiences in the group into the home.

Playgroups, which began as a minor movement, are now a major social influence. Parents help playgroups. Playgroups help parents. This exchange is a great new contribution which the playgroup movement makes within the community.

Books, films and addresses

Further reading

Axline, V. *Dibs: In Search of Self*, Penguin, Harmondsworth 1947; Ballantine, New York 1969
Bodor, J. *Creating and Presenting Hand Puppets*, Reinhold, New York 1967
Bowlby, J. *Child Care and Growth of Love*, Penguin, Harmondsworth and Baltimore 1953
Clegg, A. and Megson, B. *Children in Distress*, Penguin, Harmondsworth 1968; William Gannon, Santa Fe 1968
Crowe, B. *The Playgroup Movement*, Allen & Unwin, London 1973
Dickinson, S. (ed.) *Mother's Help*, Collins, London 1972
Dryad *Animal Glove Puppets*, Dryad Press Publications, Dryad, Northgates, Leicester
Holt, J. *How Children Learn*, Penguin, Harmondsworth 1967; Dell, New York 1972
Hostler, P. *The Child's World*, Penguin, Harmondsworth 1969
Isaacs, S. *The Nursery Years*, Routledge, London 1932; Vanguard Press, New York
Jackson, S. *Simple Puppetry*, Studio Vista, London; Watson-Guptill, New York 1972
Jameson, K. *Pre-School and Infant Art*, Studio Vista, London 1968; Viking Press, New York 1969
Molony, E. *How to Form a Playgroup*, BBC Publications, London; International Publications Service, New York 1967
Newsom, J. and E. *Four Years Old in an Urban Community*, Penguin, London 1970; Aldine Publishing Co., Chicago 1968
Roberts, V. *Playing, Learning and Living*, A. & C. Black, London 1971
Shea, K. *Liverpool and its Under-Fives*, Association of Multi-Racial Playgroups, London 1970
Van der Eyken, W. *The Pre-School Years*, Penguin, Harmondsworth 1967; Penguin, Baltimore 1968
Winnicot, D. W. *The Child, the Family and the Outside World*, Penguin, Harmondsworth 1964; Penguin, Baltimore 1970

A wide range of pamphlets is available in the UK from: The Pre-School Playgroups Association, Alford House, Aveline Street, London SE11 5DJ and The British Association for Early Childhood Education, Montgomery Hall, Harleyford Road, London SE11; and in the USA from: National Association for the Education of Young Children, 1834 Connecticut Avenue NW, Washington, DC 20009.

Picture books for the book corner

Burton, V. L. *Katy and the Big Snow*, Faber & Faber, London 1947; H.M. Goushu Co, San José

Emberley, B. and E. *Drummer Hoff*, Bodley Head, London 1970; Prentice-Hall, Englewood Cliffs 1967

Fatio, L. *The Happy Lion*, Puffin Picture Book, Penguin, Harmondsworth 1969; McGraw-Hill, New York 1954

Gramatky, H. *Hercules*, World's Work, London 1969; Putnam, New York 1971

Hewett, A. *Mrs Mopple's Washing Line*, Puffin Picture Books, Penguin 1970

Hoban, R. *A Baby Sister for Frances*, Faber & Faber, London 1970; Harper & Row, New York 1964

Hoban, R. *Bedtime for Frances*, Faber & Faber, London 1970; Harper & Row, New York 1960

Hughes, S. *Lucy and Tom's Day*, Gollancz, London 1969

Hutchins, P. *Tom and Sam*, Bodley Head, London 1969; Macmillan, New York 1968

Hutchins, P. *Titch*, Bodley Head, London 1972; Macmillan, New York 1971

Iwasaki, C. *Momoko and the Pretty Bird*, Bodley Head, London 1972

Keats, E. J. *The Snowy Day*, Bodley Head, London 1967; Viking, New York 1962

Keats, E. J. *Whistle for Willie*, Bodley Head, London 1966; Viking, New York 1964

Kent, J. *The Fat Cat*, Hamish Hamilton, London 1972; Parent's Magazine Press, New York 1971

Krasilovsky, P. *The Cow Who Fell in the Canal*, World's Work, London 1958; Doubleday, New York 1957

Piatti, C. *The Happy Owls*, Benn, London 1965; Atheneum, New York 1964

Prince, A. and Hickson, J. *Joe Moves House*, BBC and Methuen, London 1972

Prøysen, A. *Mrs Pepperpot's Christmas*, Hutchinson, London 1972

Sendak, M. *Where the Wild Things Are*, Bodley Head, London 1967; Harper & Row, New York 1963

Tolstoy, A. *The Great Big Enormous Turnip*, Heinemann, London 1968; Watts, New York 1969

Wildsmith, B. *Birds*, Oxford University Press, London; Watts, New York 1967

Wildsmith, B. *Animals*, Oxford University Press, London; Watts, New York 1957

Wildsmith, B. *Fishes*, Oxford University Press, London; Watts, New York 1968

Wildsmith, B. *Twelve Days of Christmas*, Oxford University Press, London; Watts, New York 1972

Zion, G. *Harry the Dirty Dog*, Bodley Head, London 1960; Harper & Row, New York 1956

Zion, G. and Graham, M. *No Roses for Harry!*, Bodley Head, London 1961; Scholastic Book Services, New York 1971

Many of the above are now available in paperback.
Some are also available as film strips obtainable from Weston-Woods Studios Ltd, PO Box 2, Henley, Oxon.

Stories for telling: sources

Ainsworth, R. *Lucky Dip*, Young Puffin, Penguin, Harmondsworth and Baltimore
Berg, L. *Little Pete Stories*, Young Puffin, Penguin, Harmondsworth 1970; Verry, Lawrence, New York 1964
Colwell, E. *Tell Me a Story*, Young Puffin, Penguin, Harmondsworth 1970; Penguin, Baltimore 1962
Colwell, E. *Tell Me Another Story*, Young Puffin, Penguin, Harmondsworth 1969; Penguin, Baltimore 1964
Colwell, E. *Time for a Story*, Young Puffin, Penguin, Harmondsworth and Baltimore 1970
Edwards, D. *My Naughty Little Sister*, Young Puffin, Penguin, Harmondsworth 1970

Films

The following films are available on hire from: Concord Films Council, Nacton, Ipswich, Suffolk
They are also distributed by: Images for Education, 2 South Audley Street, London W1
Growth Through Play (black and white): Film 1. *In the Beginning*. Birth to four months. Film 2. *From Hand to Mouth*. Four months to nine months. Film 3. *Moving Off*. Eight months to twelve months.
Children and . . . (black and white): *Clay, Water, Dough, Dry Sand, Wet Sand, Paint* (colour)
It is essential to read *Notes on Showing of P.P.A. Films* in order to get the best out of these ten-minute films. The notes are obtainable from Pre-School Playgroups Association, price 30p.

Film strip

Playgroups in their Communities, forty-three frames dealing with setting up a playgroup, getting advice, and organizing some activities. Obtainable from: E.P. Group of Companies, Bradford Road, East Ardsley, Wakefield, Yorks

Useful addresses

In the U.K.
Pre-School Playgroups Association, Alford House, Aveline St, London SE11
The British Association for Early Childhood Education (formerly The Nursery School Association), Montgomery Hall, Harley Ford Road, London SE11
Save the Children Fund, 29 Queen Anne's Gate, London SW1
Dryad Ltd, Northgates, Leicester, LE1 4QR
Educational Supply Association Ltd, Pinnacles, P.O. Box 22, Harlow, Essex
Galt's Ltd (toys), 30 Great Marlborough St, London W1
George Rowney Ltd, 12 Percy Street, London W1A 2BP
Her Majesty's Stationery Office, 423 Oxford Street, London W1
Margros Ltd, Monument Way West, Woking, Surrey
Paul and Marjorie Abbatt, Toys and Nursery Equipment, 328 Kennington Lane, London SE11
Reeves and Sons Ltd, 249 Lincoln Road, Enfield, Middlesex
Winsor and Newton Ltd, Wealdstone, Harrow, Middlesex

In the U.S.A.
American Institute of Child Care Centers, 2582 Sheriff Way, Winter Park, Florida 32789
American Montessori Society, 175 Fifth Avenue, New York, New York 10010
Child Craft Education Corp., 964 Third Avenue, New York, New York 10022
Creative Playthings Inc., Princeton, New Jersey 08540
Day Care and Child Development Council of America Inc., 1426 H Street NW, Washington DC 20005
Educational Facilities Laboratory (EFL), 477 Madison Avenue, New York, New York 10022
J. L. Hammett Co., 2393 Vaux Hall Road, Union, New Jersey 07083
National Association for the Education of Young Children, 1834 Connecticut Avenue NW, Washington, D.C. 20009
2001 Inc., 47 Riverside Avenue, Box 296, Saugatuck Station, Westport, Connecticut 06880

Index

Additives for paint 26
Adhesives 43
Adults 104
Ages and Stages 15
Aprons 46, 101, 102
Art and craft activities 106
Assessment 15
Barrels 96
Battery boards 82
Bean bags 97
Bit boxes 43, 76
Book corner 68
Boots 81
Bowls 102
Brushes 25, 26
Brushes, domestic 81
Bubbles 50
Bubble bowl 52
Bulb planting 88
Christmas decorations 44
Clay storage 31
Clearing up 46, 102
Climbing 57
Climbing frame 96
Clothes 76
Colour consistency 25
colour corner 86
colour, experience of 22
colour, expression of 22
colour, organization of 22
colour theory 25
Construction toys 58
Crowe, Brenda 6
Display 44
Dolls' house 80
Domestic pets 90
Dressing up 27, 74
Dressing up corner 76
Easels 25
Environment, exploration of 8
Experience 10, 24, 86
Expression 27
Extra room 104
Evidence 26
Eyken, Van der 70
Fantasy 10, 11, 54, 57, 72, 74, 106
Finger paint 26, 28

Finger paint recipe 28
Finger painting 102
Firemen 93
Flag pattern 22
Ground sheet 102
Gym mat 96
Hats 75
Home corner 72
Horse shoe 64
Imagination 11, 54
Imitation 37
Imitating sound 62
Improvised building materials 57
Inhibiting factors 25
Kaleidoscope 81
Kellogg, Rhoda 43
Local parks 93
Lines, Kathleen 70
Listening skills 60
Literary activities 106
Magnets 81
Manipulation 30
Marsh, Leonard 20
Matterson, Elizabeth 70
Mental development 89
Milk bottle crates 57
Milk-time talk 99
Mixing table 85
Mothers 107
Movement 62
Muscular control 15
Musical accessories 63
Number concept 78
Ovens 46
Paper 26
Paper towels 102
Parents 107
Pattern of development 15
Pedal cars 96
Physical activity 57, 106
Pictures 100
Plants 88
Play as play 106
Play dens 74
Playdough 98
Playdough recipe 32
Police force 93
Premises 102

Problem-solving 57
Progressions 26
Protective clothing 27
Public libraries 69
Puppets 77
Quiet corner 104
Quoits 97
Radio and TV table 83
'Real' music 64
Records 64
Reluctant painters 27
Sand play 53
Scribbles, Stage 1 13
Scribbles, Stage 2, Stage 3 15
Selotape 43
Sequences 21
Shakers 61
Singing 65
Slide 96
Smelling table 86
Snails 89
Soft toys 73
Space concept 78
Stages 20
Storage 104
Story-time 66
Stripe pattern 22
Symbols 20
Tadpoles 89
Taking work home 43
Toxicity 28
Toy-shop toys 79
Trampolines 96
Tricycles 96
Tutaev, Belle 7
Twigs 88
Tyre-trollies 96
Velcro 73, 76, 101
Visual stimulation 106
'Walter Mitty' 11
Water play 47
White Paper, H.M.S.O./5174 106
Wildsmith, Brian 70
Winchester Conference 91
Woodwork tools 36

112

DISCHARGED
DISCHARGED OCT 15 1984
DISCHARGED

DISCHARGED   DISCHARGED
   DISCHARGED
              DISCHARGED
DISCHARGED 1982   SEP 2 8 1990

       FEB 2 8 1983
         DISCHARGED

     DISCHARGED   FEB 2 5 1992
DISCHARGED

FEB 1 4 1990

FEB 1 4 1990